What's in
Daily Math Practice

36 Weekly Sections

Monday through Thursday

- two computation problems

  Addition and subtraction are practiced each week. Simple multiplication begins in week 32.

- two items that practice a variety of math skills

- one word problem

Friday

Friday's format includes one problem that is more extensive and may require multiple steps. These problems emphasize reasoning and communication in mathematics.

Also featured on Friday is a graph form where students record the number of problems they got correct each day that week.

Additional Features

Scope and Sequence

Scope and sequence charts on pages 3 and 4 detail the specific skills to be practiced and show when they will be presented. The skills included are found in math texts at this level.

Answer Key

The answer key begins on page 117.

How to Solve Word Problems Chart

Award Certificate

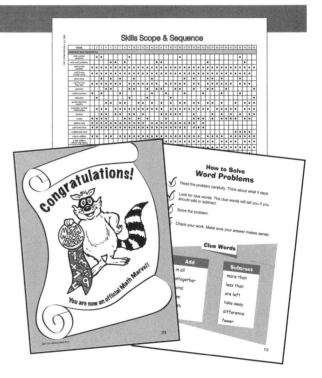

How to Use *Daily Math Practice*

You may want to use all of the following presentations throughout the year to keep each lesson fresh and interesting.

1. Make overhead transparencies of the lessons. Present each lesson as an oral activity with the entire class. Write answers and make corrections using an erasable marker.

   As the class becomes more familiar with *Daily Math Practice*, you may want students to mark their answers first and then check them against correct responses marked on the transparency.

2. Reproduce the pages for individuals or partners to work on independently. Check answers as a group, using an overhead transparency to model the correct answers. (Use these pages as independent practice only after much oral group experience with the lessons.)

3. Occasionally you may want to use a day's or even a full week's lesson(s) as a test to see how individuals are progressing in their acquisition of skills.

Some Important Considerations

1. Allow students to use whatever tools they need to solve problems. Some students will choose to use manipulatives, while others will want to make drawings.

2. It is important that students be able to share their solutions. This modeling of a variety of problem-solving techniques provides a great learning benefit. Don't scrimp on the amount of time you allow for discussing how solutions were reached.

Suggestions and Options

1. Sometimes you will not have taught a given skill before it appears in a lesson. These items should then be done together. Tell the class that you are going to work on a skill they have not yet been taught. Use the practice time to conduct a minilesson on that skill.

2. Customize the daily lessons to the needs of your class.

   • If there are skills that are not included in the grade-level expectancies of the particular program you teach, you may choose to skip those items.

   • If you feel your class needs more practice than is provided, add these "extras" on your own in the form of a one-item warm-up or posttest.

Skills Scope & Sequence

Week	1	2	3	4	5	6	7	8	9	10	11	12	13	14	15	16	17	18	19	20	21	22	23	24	25	26	27	28	29	30	31	32	33	34	35	36
Number and Operations																																				
write number sentences		•	•						•											•													•			
write word problems					•	•		•																		•								•		
read & write numbers	•		•	•	•	•	•	•	•	•	•	•	•	•	•	•	•	•		•	•	•	•	•	•	•	•	•	•	•	•	•	•	•	•	•
read & write number words	•		•	•	•	•	•		•	•	•	•	•	•	•	•	•	•	•	•	•	•	•	•	•	•	•	•	•	•	•	•	•	•	•	
place value			•		•		•						•	•							•		•										•			
count by twos, fives, tens	•		•		•		•		•	•		•			•	•	•		•	•				•		•	•		•		•		•	•	•	
odd/even				•	•				•	•						•				•										•						•
ordinal numbers	•		•				•							•			•				•				•				•				•			
estimation		•							•				•					•																		•
greater/less than, equal to				•	•		•	•			•							•					•	•			•		•			•		•	•	
properties, number relationships			•	•		•				•	•	•		•		•	•		•	•	•	•	•	•	•	•	•		•	•	•	•				•
fractions							•			•		•	•				•	•	•	•		•	•				•	•	•	•	•				•	
money	•		•	•							•	•		•		•	•				•	•	•		•				•						•	
addition facts	•	•	•	•		•	•	•		•	•	•		•	•	•	•			•	•	•	•		•	•										
subtraction facts	•	•	•	•																•				•	•											
multiplication facts																																			•	•
column addition	•	•			•	•	•				•				•					•						•	•	•	•	•	•	•	•	•	•	•
2-digit addition without regrouping				•		•							•	•	•									•		•	•	•	•	•	•	•	•	•	•	•
2-digit addition with regrouping							•																•	•		•	•	•	•	•	•	•	•	•	•	•
2-digit subtraction without regrouping													•				•	•		•			•			•	•	•	•	•	•	•	•	•	•	
2-digit subtraction with regrouping																							•		•	•	•	•	•	•	•	•	•	•	•	
3-digit addition & subtraction																					•				•				•					•	•	•
solve word problems	•	•	•	•	•	•	•	•	•	•	•	•	•	•	•	•	•	•	•	•	•	•	•	•	•	•	•	•	•	•	•	•	•	•	•	•

Week	1	2	3	4	5	6	7	8	9	10	11	12	13	14	15	16	17	18	19	20	21	22	23	24	25	26	27	28	29	30	31	32	33	34	35	36
Algebra																																				
sort and classify	•											•																					•			
name and extend patterns		•					•	•	•					•				•	•		•			•		•		•	•	•	•	•				•
simple number patterns			•								•			•				•				•							•		•				•	
Geometry																																				
shapes	•	•		•	•	•		•			•	•	•				•					•		•	•			•	•	•		•	•	•	•	•
symmetry and congruence					•			•					•					•							•					•			•			
directions about direction										•									•																	
Measurement																																				
perimeter			•						•					•						•								•								
weight and capacity			•			•	•			•						•							•					•				•				
time		•			•	•	•			•		•		•	•	•		•	•	•	•	•		•	•	•		•		•	•	•	•	•	•	•
linear measure					•			•												•							•							•		•
Data Analysis and Probability																																				
read and interpret graphs	•																•											•								
create graphs													•																	•						
use tally marks	•			•	•										•		•								•					•			•			
probability																																•			•	

1. twelve + four = _____

4. 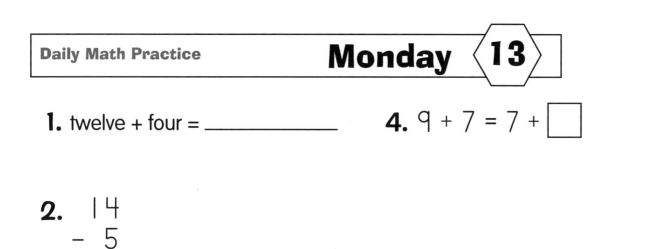 $9 + 7 = 7 +$ ☐

2.   14
    − 5

3.

= _____ ¢

5. Jim saw 8 sea lions yesterday and 7 today. How many sea lions did Jim see?

_____ sea lions

---

1. 12 − 12 = _____

4. Mark the odd numbers.

 1 2 3 4 5 6 7 8 9

2.   13
    − 7

3. Mark the cone.

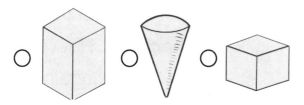

5. There were 15 pigeons on the roof. If 8 flew away, how many were left?

_____ pigeons

1. 17 – 0 = _____

2.   12
   +14
   ____

3. Draw a line to make two sides that are the same.

Dog

4. 108 _____ _____

   _____ 112

5. How far will Alana travel if she walks six miles today and nine miles tomorrow?

   _____ miles

1. 7 + 6 + 2 = _____

2.   28
   – 11
   ____

3. About how many pennies will this jar hold?

   a. 500   b. 25   c. 150

4. Circle the object that is the same size and shape.

5. There are 4 apple trees, 7 pear trees, and 4 apricot trees in Ryan's backyard. How many fruit trees are there altogether?

   _____ trees

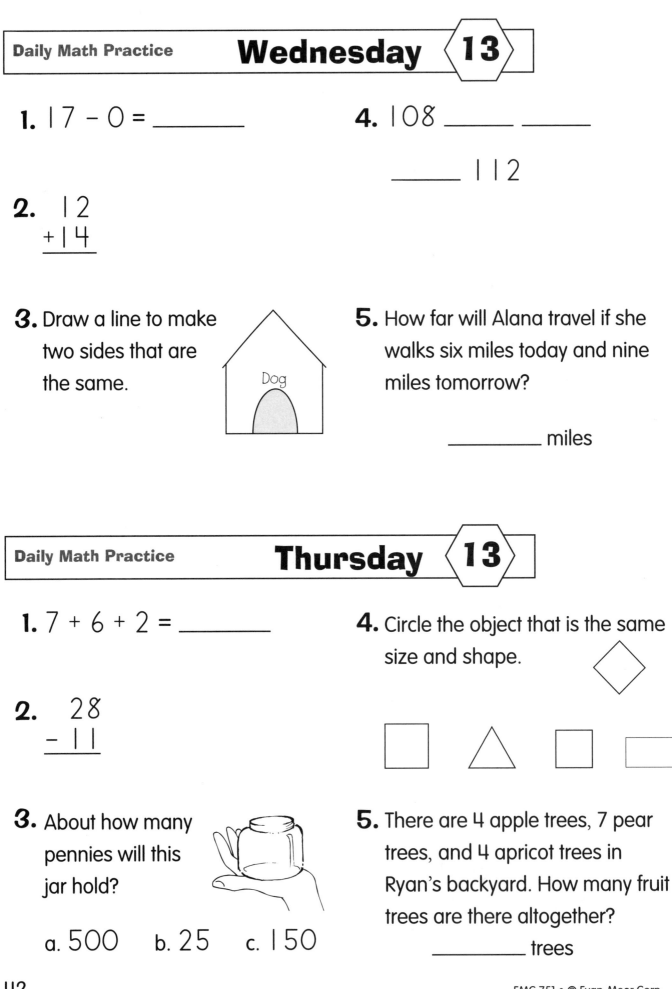

Friday  13

Elephants

	1	2	5
trunk	1		
ears	2		
feet	4		
tail	1		

Daily Progress Record 13

How many did you get correct each day? Color the squares.

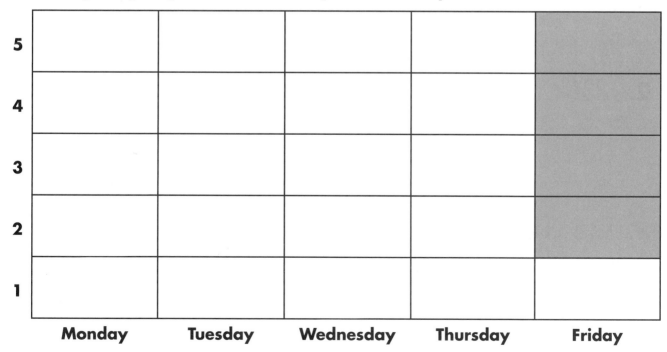

1. $5 + 8 - 6 =$ _____

2. $17 - 7 =$ _____

3. How many feet around the pool?

6 feet

3 feet   3 feet

6 feet   _____ feet

4. $11 \boxed{} 2 = 13$

5. Recess is 15 minutes long. Ben and Tara have been playing for 8 minutes. How much longer can they play?

_____ minutes

1. $16 - 7 =$ _____

2. $\begin{array}{r} 32 \\ +\ 5 \\ \hline \end{array}$

3. Make an **X** on the fourth slipper.

4. $12 + 4 = 16$, so

$16 - 4 = \boxed{}$

5. Grandma planted 4 rows of squash, 2 rows of beans, and 7 rows of corn in her garden. How many rows did she plant?

_____ rows

44

1. $9 + 3 + 5 =$ _____

2. $11 - 7 =$ _____

3.

$=$ _____

4. Name the pattern.

_____

5. The petting zoo had 6 goats, 2 sheep, 1 pony, and 1 calf. How many animals were in the petting zoo?

_____ animals

1. $15 - 8 - 7 =$ _____

2. $\begin{array}{r} 10 \\ +\ 2 \\ \hline \end{array}$

3. Write the time.

half past _____

4. Fill in the correct symbol.

$< = >$

$4 + 5 \bigcirc 6 - 2$

5. Emma picked twelve flowers. She put ten in a vase. How many flowers were left?

_____ flowers

Jill has three pairs of shoes. Jay has three pairs, too. How many shoes do they have in all?

_____ shoes

Daily Math Practice

Daily Progress Record ⟨14⟩

How many did you get correct each day? Color the squares.

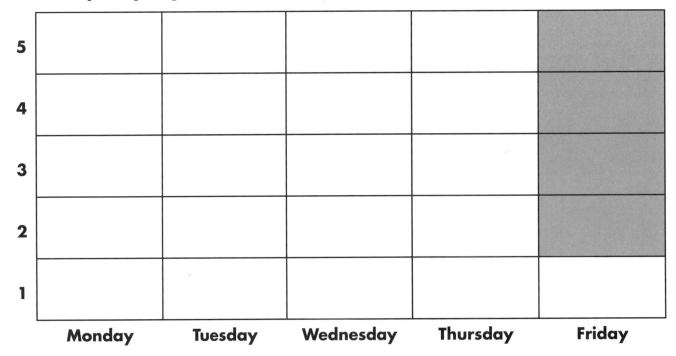

	Monday	Tuesday	Wednesday	Thursday	Friday
5					
4					
3					
2					
1					

1. $9 + 7 =$ _____

2. $\begin{array}{r} 29 \\ -\ 17 \\ \hline \end{array}$

3. Mark number nineteen.

  9   29   19

4. Look at the clocks. How many minutes have passed?

_____ minutes

5. Ronnie gathered 9 white eggs and 6 brown eggs. How many eggs did she have?

_____ eggs

1. $19 - 5 =$ _____

2. $\begin{array}{r} 8 \\ 3 \\ +\ 4 \\ \hline \end{array}$

3. $6 + 5 = 11$, so

  $5 + 6 = \boxed{}$

4. 7 is an even number.

  yes   no

5. Write a word problem for $15 - 8 = 7$.

_____

_____

_____

1. $13 - 6 =$ _____

2.
$$43$$
$$+ \ 6$$

3. Count by ones.

$$110 \ \rule{1cm}{0.4pt} \ \rule{1cm}{0.4pt} \ \rule{1cm}{0.4pt}$$

4. Use tally marks to show 29.

5. Ali went to the zoo on his birthday. He asked 14 friends to go with him. If 3 couldn't go, how many friends went with him?

_____ friends

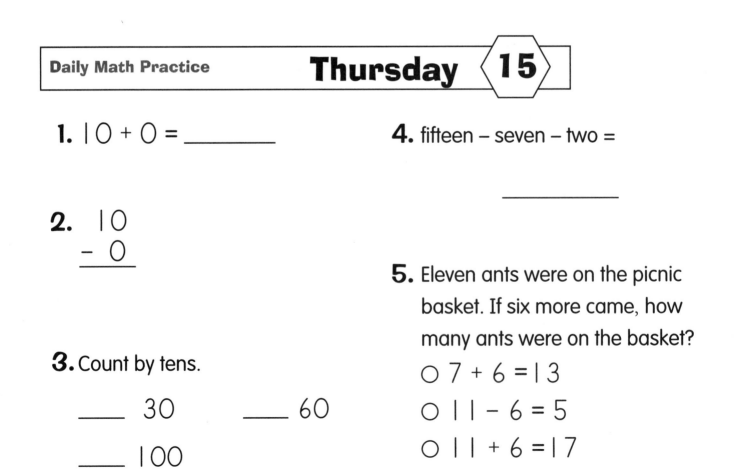

Daily Math Practice   **Thursday** 15

1. $10 + 0 =$ _____

2.
$$10$$
$$- \ 0$$

3. Count by tens.

____ 30   ____ 60

____ 100

4. fifteen – seven – two =

_____

5. Eleven ants were on the picnic basket. If six more came, how many ants were on the basket?

○ $7 + 6 = 13$

○ $11 - 6 = 5$

○ $11 + 6 = 17$

Make each line add up to 6.

across ➡
down ⬇
corner to corner ⬂

Magic Square

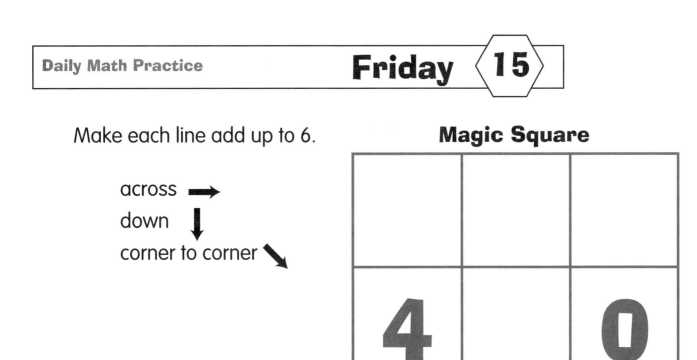

Daily Math Practice

Daily Progress Record 〈15〉

How many did you get correct each day? Color the squares.

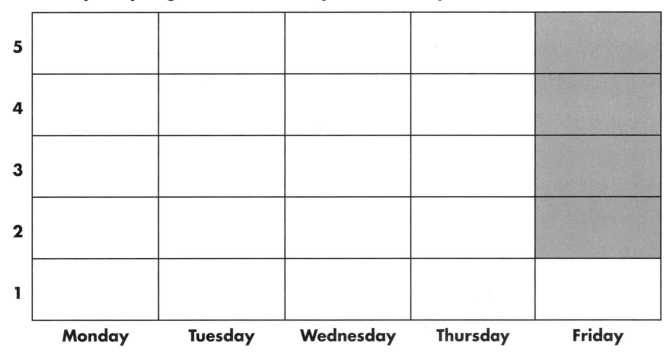

1. 5 + 6 + 3 = _____

2.   14
       – 5

3. Circle the tool that you would use to weigh the rabbit:

4. Write eighteen.

_____

5. Annie saw 9 yellow and black moths and 6 white moths. How many moths did she see?

_____ moths

1. 13 – 6 = _____

2.   21
       + 18

3. Color $\frac{1}{3}$.

4. Fill in the correct symbol.

< = >

96 ◯ 69

5. Serena collected 18 rocks and shells. If she has 7 rocks, how many shells does she have?

_____ shells

1. 15 – 8 = _____

2.   6
  + 7
  ‾‾‾‾

3. What time is it?

   4:45

   a quarter to _____

4. 9 is odd.

   yes   no

5. Write a word problem for

   16 – 7 = 9.

   _____

   _____

   _____

1. thirteen – seven = _____

2. 7 + 7 = _____

3. 9 + 8 = 17, so

   17 – 9 = ☐

4. 11 – ☐ = 5

5. Kelly has a dozen stickers. If she gives the stickers to six of her friends, how many will each friend get?

   _____ stickers

Friday ⟨16⟩

Nadia and Bo picked vegetables from the garden.
They filled 2 baskets with vegetables. Each basket
had 5 ears of corn, 4 tomatoes, and 3 squash.

How many vegetables were in one basket?

_____ vegetables

How many vegetables were in two baskets?

_____ vegetables

Daily Progress Record ⟨16⟩

How many did you get correct each day? Color the squares.

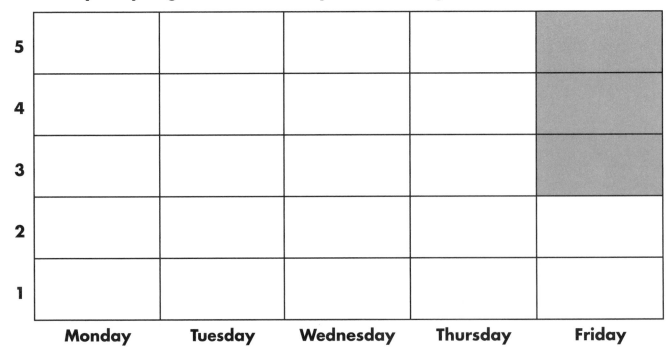

	Monday	Tuesday	Wednesday	Thursday	Friday
5					
4					
3					
2					
1					

1. $7 + 8 =$ _____

2.
$$\begin{array}{r} 10 \\ -\ 3 \\ \hline \end{array}$$

3. Make an **X** on the seventh balloon.

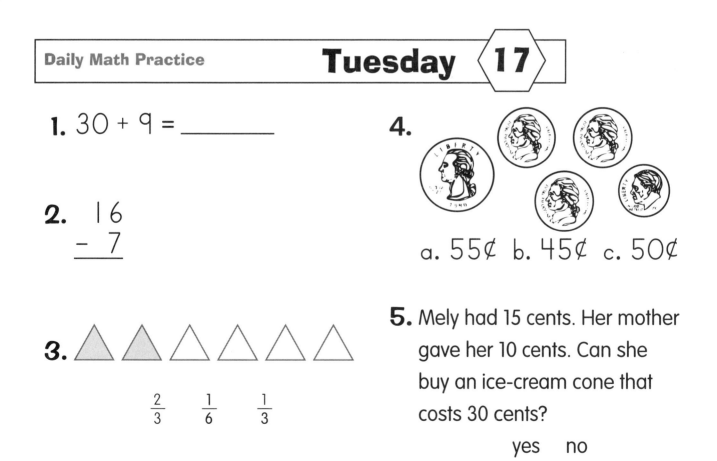

4. How much?

//// //// //// /

_____

5. Milton has two brothers and four sisters. How many children are in Milton's family?

_____ children

1. $30 + 9 =$ _____

2.
$$\begin{array}{r} 16 \\ -\ 7 \\ \hline \end{array}$$

3.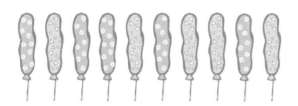

$\frac{2}{3}$ $\frac{1}{6}$ $\frac{1}{3}$

4.

a. 55¢ b. 45¢ c. 50¢

5. Mely had 15 cents. Her mother gave her 10 cents. Can she buy an ice-cream cone that costs 30 cents?

yes   no

1. $8 + 9 =$ _____

4. twenty – fourteen = _____

2. $\begin{array}{r} 25 \\ -\ 3 \\ \hline \end{array}$

3. What comes before?

_____97   _____100

_____131   _____160

5. There are 15 kids on my block that have blue bikes and 4 kids that have red bikes. How many kids have bikes?

○ $1 + 5 + 4 =$

○ $15 + 4 =$

○ $15 - 4 =$

Daily Math Practice **Thursday** ⟨**17**⟩

1. $24 + 2 =$ _____

4. Count by fives.

___ ___ 15 ___ ___ 30

2. $\begin{array}{r} 14 \\ -\ 9 \\ \hline \end{array}$

3. Mark the cube.

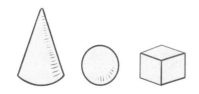

5. Wes has 30¢ in his bank. He has 20¢ in his pocket. He found 30¢ under the sofa. How much money does Wes have?

less than $1 $1   more than $1

Which Toy Do You Like Best?

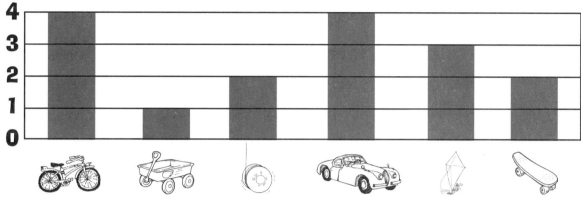

Look at the graph. What does it tell you?

I can tell:

1. _____

2. _____

How many did you get correct each day? Color the squares.

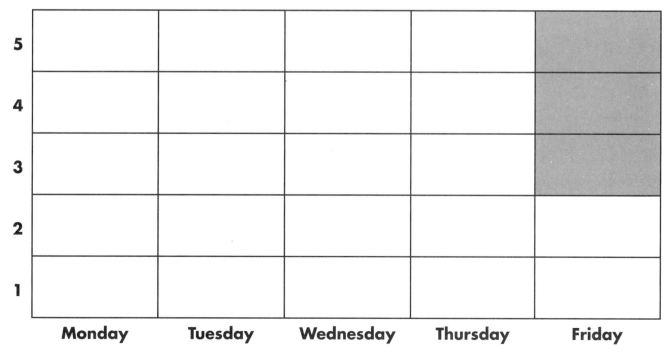

Monday 18

1. $8 + 8 =$ _____

2. $\begin{array}{r} 67 \\ -\ 5 \\ \hline \end{array}$

3. What time is it?

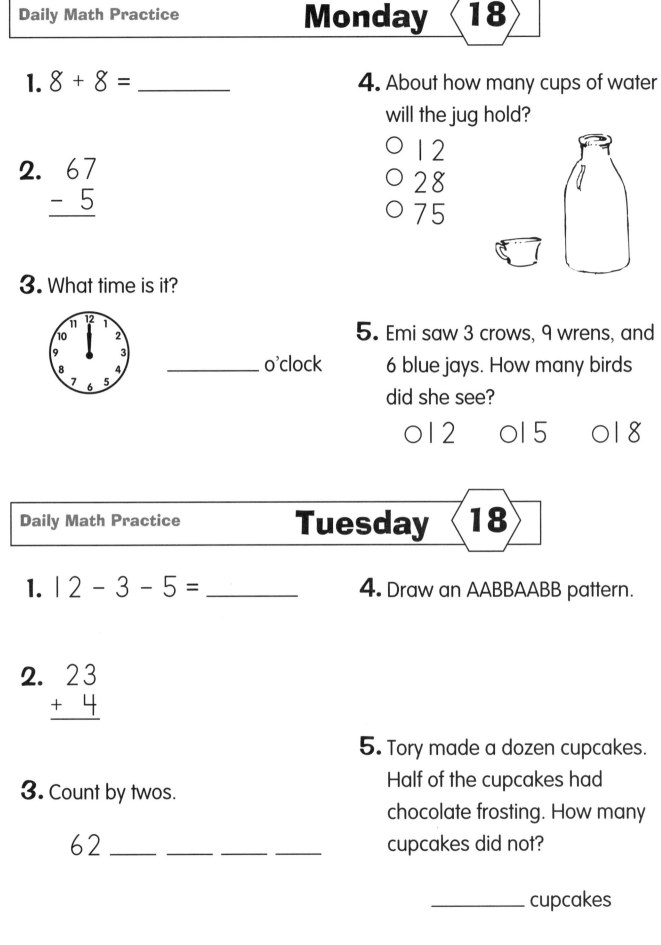

_____ o'clock

4. About how many cups of water will the jug hold?

○ 12
○ 28
○ 75

5. Emi saw 3 crows, 9 wrens, and 6 blue jays. How many birds did she see?

○ 12　　○ 15　　○ 18

Tuesday 18

1. $12 - 3 - 5 =$ _____

2. $\begin{array}{r} 23 \\ +\ 4 \\ \hline \end{array}$

3. Count by twos.

62 ___ ___ ___ ___

4. Draw an AABBAABB pattern.

5. Tory made a dozen cupcakes. Half of the cupcakes had chocolate frosting. How many cupcakes did not?

_____ cupcakes

1. $6 + 8 + 3 =$ _____

2. $\begin{array}{r} 17 \\ -\ 9 \\ \hline \end{array}$

3. Which container holds just 4 cups of milk?

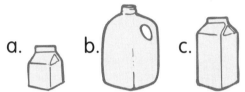

a. b. c.

4. Fill in the correct symbol.

$$< \ = \ >$$

$8 + 7 \ \bigcirc \ 12 - 3$

5. Connie saw 18 birds in a tree. Then 5 birds flew away. How many are still in the tree? How can you find the answer?

a. +   b. −   c. x

---

1. $12 + 7 =$ _____

2. $\begin{array}{r} 18 \\ -\ 9 \\ \hline \end{array}$

3. Are both sides the same?

yes   no

4. $11 \ \square \ 6 = 17$

5. If the teacher asks each student to talk for 5 minutes about a hobby, how long would it take for 8 students to talk?

a. 13 minutes

b. 3 minutes

c. 40 minutes

Friday 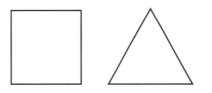 18

Use these two shapes to make an ABBABBABB pattern.

Daily Progress Record ⟨18⟩

How many did you get correct each day? Color the squares.

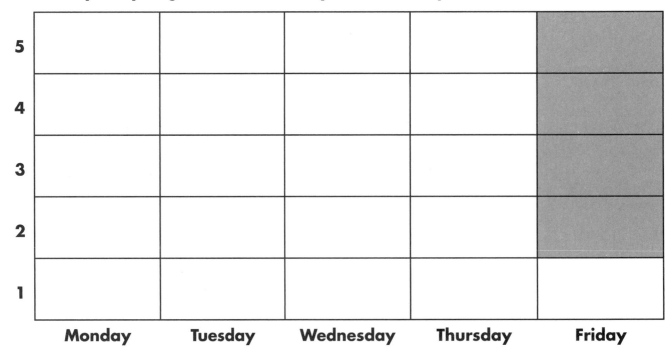

	Monday	Tuesday	Wednesday	Thursday	Friday
5					
4					
3					
2					
1					

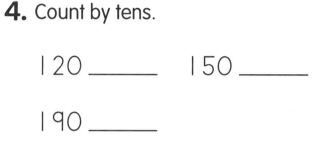

1. 5 + 8 + 3 = _____

2. 12
     − 5

3. What comes next?

89 _____   75 _____

129 _____   111 _____

4. Count by tens.

120 _____   150 _____

190 _____

5. Marcus needs 18¢ for a pen. If he has 12¢, how much more does he need?

_____¢

Daily Math Practice **Tuesday** 19

1. 16 − 7 = _____

2. 5
     + 9

3. Mark $\frac{1}{2}$.

4. twenty − fourteen =

_____

5. Mrs. Reyes has worked at the store for 18 years. Mr. Lee has worked there for 9 years. How much longer has Mrs. Reyes worked at the store?

_____ years

1. $7 + 6 =$ _____

2. $\begin{array}{r} 17 \\ -\ 8 \\ \hline \end{array}$

3. Number in order from heavy to light.

____   ____   ____

4. $12 + 12 = 24$, so

 $- 12 = 12$

5. Ray spent 25¢ on ice cream and 40¢ for a cold drink. How much did he spend?

_____ ¢

---

1. $14 - 9 =$ _____

2. $\begin{array}{r} 46 \\ +\ 23 \\ \hline \end{array}$

3. Name the pattern.

_____

4. 3 is even.

yes   no

5. Ramon has stamps from many lands. He has 18 stamps from Mexico and 9 stamps from the USA. How many more Mexican stamps does he have?

_____ stamps

Friday ⟨19⟩

Begin at the star. Where is each object located?

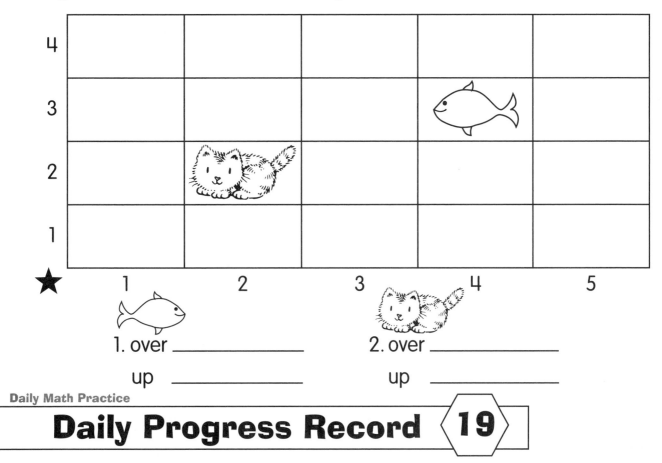

1. over _____

up _____

2. over _____

up _____

Daily Progress Record ⟨19⟩

How many did you get correct each day? Color the squares.

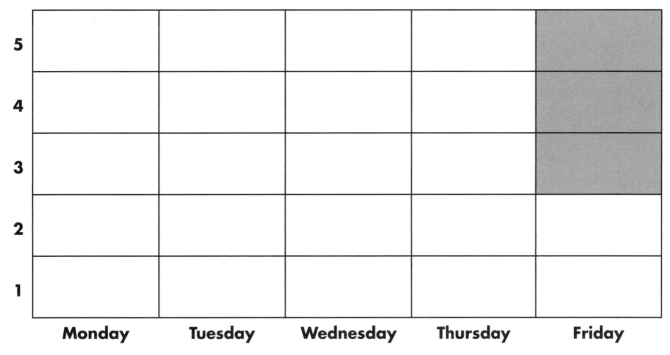

1. $17 - 9 =$ _____

2. $\begin{array}{r} 75 \\ + 14 \\ \hline \end{array}$

3. Count by twos.

88 _____   66 _____

44 _____

4. Fill in the correct symbol.

< = >

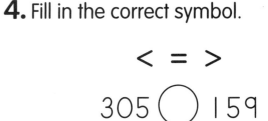
305 ◯ 159

5. There are 13 students that walk to school and 5 students that ride the bus. How many more walk?

_____ students

---

1. $14 + 10 + 4 =$ _____

2. eleven − eight = _____

3. How long is the straw?

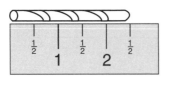

_____ inches

4. $12 +$ ☐ $= 24$

5. Write four number sentences using 8, 9, and 17.

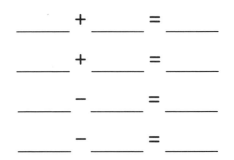

_____ + _____ = _____

_____ + _____ = _____

_____ − _____ = _____

_____ − _____ = _____

1. $14 - 7 - 3 =$ _____

2.
$$\begin{array}{r} 11 \\ + \ 8 \\ \hline \end{array}$$

3. How far is it around this shape?

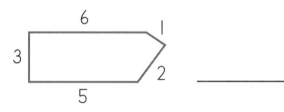

_____

4. Mark the odd numbers.

6   9   3   2

5. The salesman had 17 toy cars. He sold 3 green cars and 6 blue cars. How many did he have left?

_____ toy cars

---

1. $18 + 0 =$ _____

2.
$$\begin{array}{r} 15 \\ - 13 \\ \hline \end{array}$$

3. Write half past three on the clock.

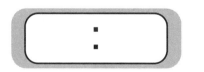

4. Color $\frac{1}{4}$.

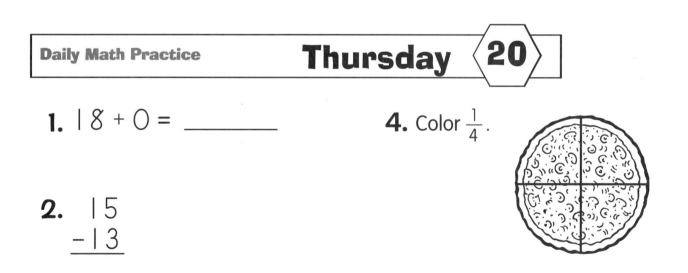

5. There are saddles for half of the 18 horses in the barn. How many saddles are there?

_____ saddles

Mr. Lee's class is building bat houses. Each group of students needs a hammer, 10 nails, and 4 pieces of lumber.

If there are 5 groups, how many hammers, nails, and pieces of lumber will be needed?

_____ hammers   _____ nails

_____ pieces of lumber

Daily Math Practice

Daily Progress Record 20

How many did you get correct each day? Color the squares.

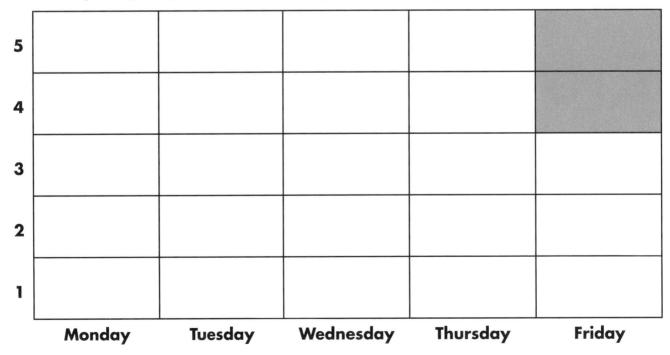

	Monday	Tuesday	Wednesday	Thursday	Friday
5					
4					
3					
2					
1					

1. 13 – 8 = _____

2. 12
    + 12
    ____

3. Make an **X** on the fourth candy cane.

🍬🍬🍬🍬🍬🍬🍬🍬

4. Fill in the correct symbol.

< = >

eight ◯ six + two

5. Cody needs a new T-shirt. He has $15. If the T-shirt costs $12, how much change will he get back?

$_____

1. 16 – 9 = _____

2. 23
    + 15
    ____

3. Write the numbers in order.

20 35 40 25 30

____ ____ ____ ____ ____

4. What time is it?

[7:15]

◯ quarter to 7
◯ quarter past 7
◯ 7 o'clock

5. Marla bought six paper hats, six balloons, and six place mats. How many friends will be at her party?

_____ friends

1. 7 + 0 + 5 = _____

2. 117
   − 17

3. Name the pattern.

_____

4. Fill in the correct symbol.

< = >

10 + 8 ◯ 9 + 10

5. Write four names for 13.

_____   _____

_____   _____

1. 13 + 10 = _____

2. 36
   − 12

3. ____ tens and ____ ones = ____

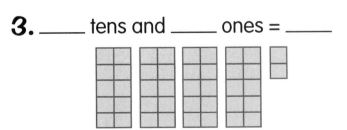

4. How many dimes are in 80¢?

_____ dimes

5. How many mittens are in nine pairs?

○ less than 10
○ more than 10
○ more than 20

66   EMC 751 • © Evan-Moor Corp.

How Many Fingers?

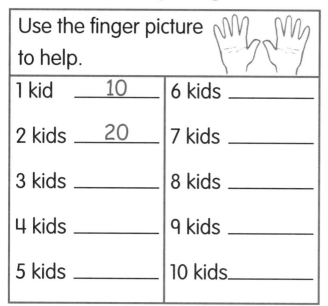

Use the finger picture to help.	
1 kid ___10___	6 kids _____
2 kids ___20___	7 kids _____
3 kids _____	8 kids _____
4 kids _____	9 kids _____
5 kids _____	10 kids_____

What pattern do you see?

_____

Daily Math Practice

Daily Progress Record 〈21〉

How many did you get correct each day? Color the squares.

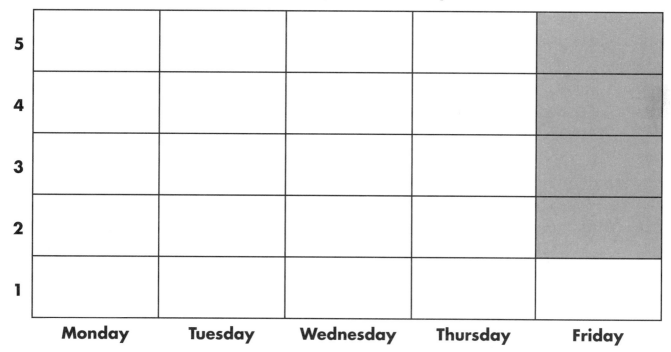

	Monday	Tuesday	Wednesday	Thursday	Friday
5					
4					
3					
2					
1					

Monday 22

1. $9 + 8 =$ _____

2. $\begin{array}{r} 219 \\ -\ 106 \\ \hline \end{array}$

3. Write the numbers in order.

9   11   6   3   20

___ ___ ___ ___ ___

4. How many eggs are in a dozen?

12   18   10

5.

1 hour ago	now	1 hour later
	3:15	
	7:45	
	11:30	

Tuesday 22

1. $19 - 9 =$ _____

2. $\begin{array}{r} 50¢ \\ +\ 20¢ \\ \hline \end{array}$

3. Mark the sphere.

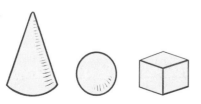

4. Draw a shape with 4 sides and 4 corners.

5. Dad cooked 15 hot dogs and 23 hamburgers for the picnic. How many pieces of meat did he cook in all?

a. 38   b. 56   c. 37

1. $18 - 6 - 3 =$ _____

2. 164
   + 230

3. What time is it?

_____ : _____

4. $100 + 0 = 100$, so

$100 - \boxed{} = 100$

5. Julie spent 20¢, Joe spent 25¢, and Bill spent 32¢. How much did they spend altogether?

_____ ¢

Daily Math Practice **Thursday** 22

1. $9 + 6 + 3 =$ _____

2. 158
   − 114

3. $6 + 9 = 15$, so

$9 + 6 = \boxed{}$

4. $12 \boxed{} 3 = 9$

5. Eight books were on the bottom shelf. Five books were on the second shelf. Four books were on the top shelf. How many books were there in all?

_____ books

Friday  22

How many squares can you count?

_____ squares

Daily Progress Record 22

How many did you get correct each day? Color the squares.

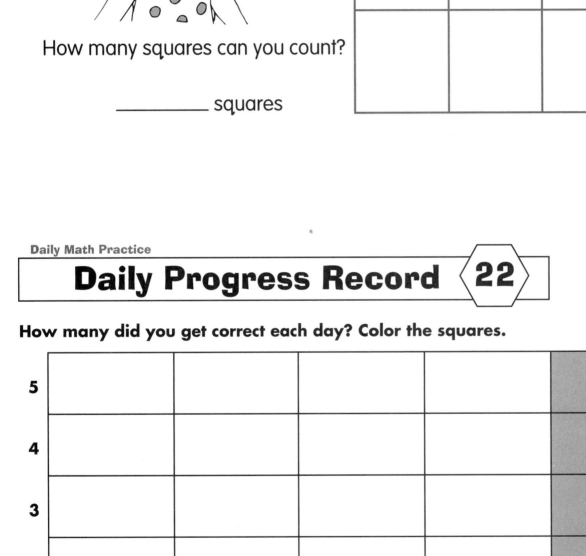

	Monday	Tuesday	Wednesday	Thursday	Friday
5					
4					
3					
2					
1					

70

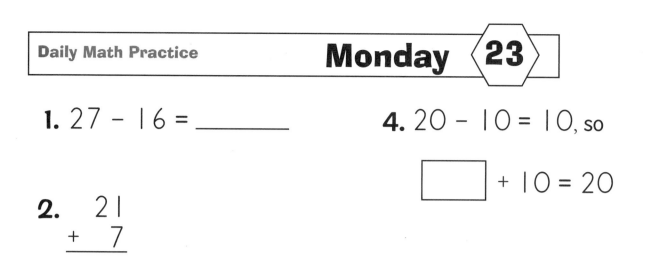

1. 27 − 16 = _____

2.   21
    + 7

3. Mark the even numbers.

     4   7   1   10

4. 20 − 10 = 10, so

   ☐ + 10 = 20

5. Inez needs 90¢ to buy a jar of paste. She has 50¢. How much more money does Inez need?

     _____¢

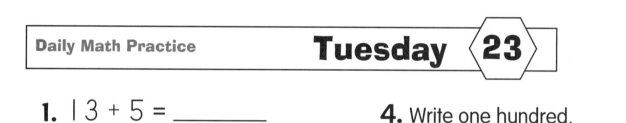

1. 13 + 5 = _____

2.   52
   + 26

3. Count by twos.

   100   102 _____ _____

4. Write one hundred.

     _____

5. A spider has eight legs. If the spider wore shoes, how many pairs would it need?

     _____ pairs of shoes

1. 90 + 6 = _____

2. 14
－ 3

3.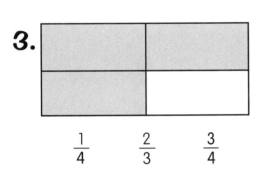

$\frac{1}{4}$ $\frac{2}{3}$ $\frac{3}{4}$

4. 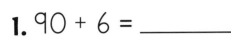 = _____ ¢

5. Yoshi saw frogs eating insects. One frog ate 7 insects, one ate 6, and another ate 5. How many insects did the frogs eat?

_____ insects

1. 60 – 20 = _____

2. 25
+ 12

3. Fill in the correct symbol.

< = >

4. 8 tens and 7 ones is _____.

5. Mr. Garcia has a lot of animals. He has three dogs, six cats, two hamsters, and five birds. How many animals does he have?

_____ animals

Fill in the chart.

How many coins do you need?

9¢		1	4
11¢			
16¢			
24¢			

Daily Math Practice

Daily Progress Record 23

How many did you get correct each day? Color the squares.

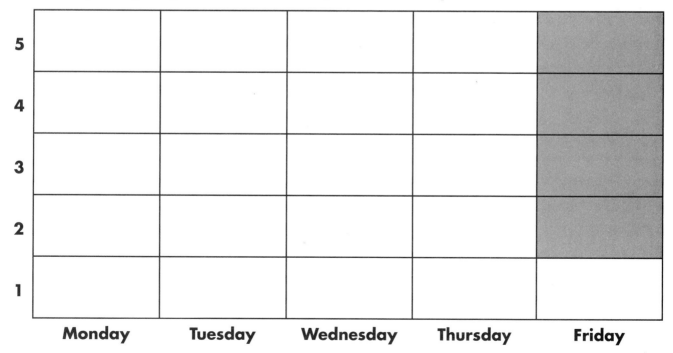

	Monday	Tuesday	Wednesday	Thursday	Friday
5					
4					
3					
2					
1					

1. 26 − 5 = _____

2.
```
  12
  15
+ 21
```

3. Count by tens.

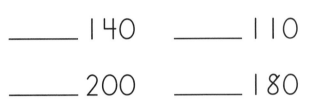

_____ 140   _____ 110

_____ 200   _____ 180

4. 15 − 12 + 6 = _____

5. The tall circus clown asked 6 children to feed the elephant 3 peanuts each. How many peanuts did the elephant eat?

○ 63   ○ 9   ○ 18

---

1. 26¢ + 15¢ = _____

2.
```
  20
−  8
```

3.
```
   nine
   two
   three
+  one
```

4. Write nineteen.

_____

5. It is 2:00. It takes Johan 30 minutes to walk home from the park. What time will he get home?

1. 17 − 7 = _____

2.   416
       + 130
       _____

3. How many sides?

_____

How many corners?

_____

4. Fill in the correct symbol.

< = >

twelve ◯ two

5. How many hippos are there if 15 are on the riverbank and 7 are in the water?

_____ hippos

1. 18 − 6 − 3 = _____

2.   30
        15
       + 21
       _____

3. Draw an AABAAB pattern.

4. 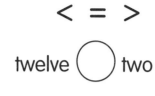 = _____

5. Today 29 monkeys escaped from the zoo. So far 16 have been caught. How many monkeys are still loose?

_____ monkeys

Paul has 40 marbles. Carmen has 10 more marbles than Paul. Albert has 10 more than Carmen.

How many marbles does Albert have?

_____ marbles

How many more marbles does Albert have than Paul?

_____ marbles

Daily Math Practice

Daily Progress Record 24

How many did you get correct each day? Color the squares.

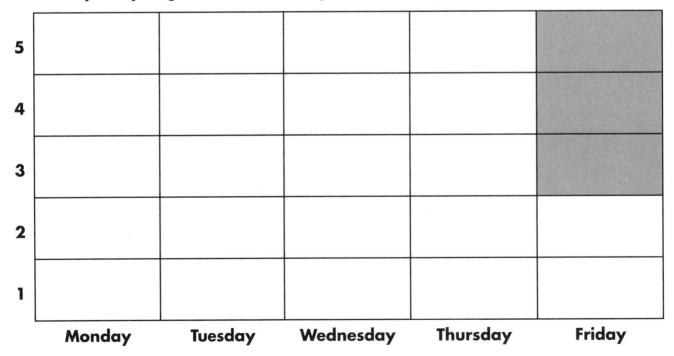

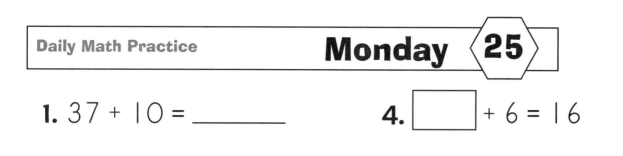

1. 37 + 10 = _____

4. [　　] + 6 = 16

2. 218
      –   6
      _____

3. Write the numbers in order.

169 167 170 166 168

____ ____ ____ ____ ____

5. Glenn's grandfather is 56 years old. His brother is 12 years old. How much older is Glenn's grandfather?

_____ years

---

1. 30 + 50 = _____

4. 1 hour = ____ minutes

2. 45
      – 14
      _____

3. Mark the words that tell how you can measure milk.

gallon   foot   liter
pound   quart   meter

5. Joan put 37¢ into her piggy bank. She took out 2 nickels and 3 pennies. How much money is left in Joan's bank?

_____ ¢

1. 16 - 2 - 8 = _____

2.   15
     + 16
     ____

3. How are these objects different?

○ different shape   ○ different color
○ different size   ○ they are the same

4. Write zero.

_____

5. The picnic started at 3:15. It lasted for three hours. Show what time it ended.

1. 16 - 11 = _____

2.   233
     + 420
     ____

3.

Which is first? _____
Which is last? _____

4. Make 32 tally marks.

5. Penny's pet hen laid an egg a day for two weeks. How many eggs did the hen lay?

_____ eggs

   EMC 751 • © Evan-Moor Corp.

Friday 25

Complete the chart. Write the letter of each object in the correct box.

SPHERE	CIRCLE

A   B   C

D   E   F

Now draw one more object in each box.

Daily Progress Record 25

How many did you get correct each day? Color the squares.

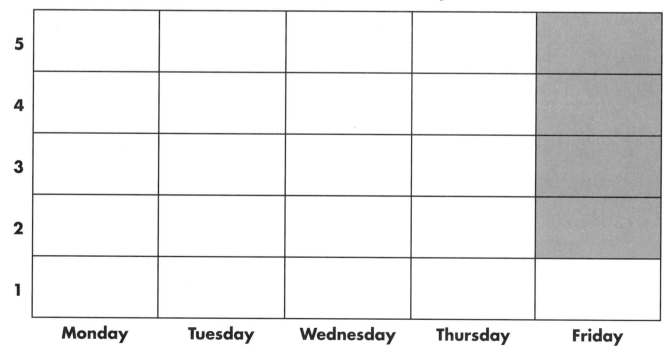

	Monday	Tuesday	Wednesday	Thursday	Friday
5					
4					
3					
2					
1					

1. $25 - 15 =$ _____

2. $\begin{array}{r} 19 \\ + \ 9 \\ \hline \end{array}$

3. Write an odd number.

_____

4. Fill in the correct symbol.

< = >

sixteen ◯ nineteen

5. If Willie has 23 chickens in a pen and 11 escape, how many chickens will still be in the pen?

_____ chickens

1. $24 + 43 =$ _____

2. $\begin{array}{r} 33 \\ - 16 \\ \hline \end{array}$

3. What time is it?

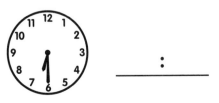 _____:_____

4. $64 =$ ____ tens and ____ ones

5. There are 36 boys and 23 girls in second grade. How many more boys are there?

_____ more boys

Wednesday ⟨**26**⟩

1. $8 + 8 + 4 + 4 =$ _____

4. $30 - \boxed{} = 20$

2. $\begin{array}{r} 35 \\ -\ 0 \\ \hline \end{array}$

5. Write a word problem for $15 + 5$.

_____

_____

_____

3. Count by fives.

75 ___ ___ ___ ___

Thursday ⟨**26**⟩

1. $15 + 10 + 14 =$ _____

4. $16 + 4 = 20$, so

$20 - 4 = \boxed{}$

2. $\begin{array}{r} 68 \\ -28 \\ \hline \end{array}$

5. Maizie made 3 cakes. She put 7 candles on each cake. How many candles did she use?

3. Write the next numbers in the pattern.

$2\ \ 5\ \ 8\ \ 11$ ___ ___

○ 0   ○ 21   ○ 17

Friday ⟨26⟩

Draw an AABCAABC pattern.

Daily Math Practice

Daily Progress Record ⟨26⟩

How many did you get correct each day? Color the squares.

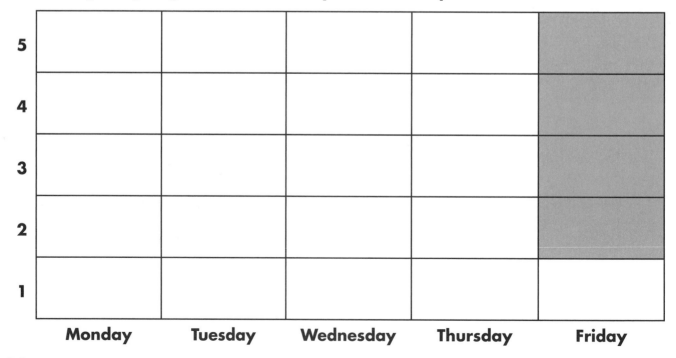

	Monday	Tuesday	Wednesday	Thursday	Friday
5					
4					
3					
2					
1					

EMC 751 • © Evan-Moor Corp.

1. 20 + 60 + 10 = _____

2.   875
       − 452

3. Fill in the correct symbol.

< = >

216 ◯ 261

4. Match:

eighteen	20
thirteen	18
twenty	12
twelve	13

5. Herbert has 21 baseball cards. If he buys 13 more, how many cards will he have?

_____ cards

1. 5,893 + 0 = _____

2.   426
       + 231

3. Name the shape.

_____

4. Write an even number.

_____

5. Megan spent 35¢ on chips and 50¢ on a cold drink. How much did her snack cost?

_____¢

1. 6 + 12 + 10 = _____

2. 20
－ 8

3. How much of this pie has been eaten?

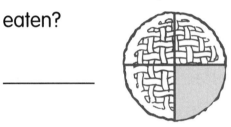

_____

4. 1 hundred + 2 tens + 0 ones =

_____

5. Max was paid 75¢ for walking Mrs. Lee's dogs. He gave Bob 35¢ for helping him. How much money did Max have left?

_____¢

---

1. 294 – 294 = _____

2. 53
+ 28

3. How long is the pencil?

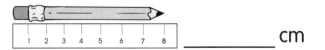 _____ cm

4. Which is the most money?
○ 4 dimes
○ 6 nickels
○ 2 quarters

5. If one pair of roller skates has 8 wheels, how many wheels will two pairs of skates have?

_____ wheels

          EMC 751 • © Evan-Moor Corp.

Friday 27

Start with 1 dozen. _____

Take away the sides of a  . − _____

Take away the number of legs on a goat. − _____

Add the corners on a ☐ . + _____
_____

How many do you have? _____

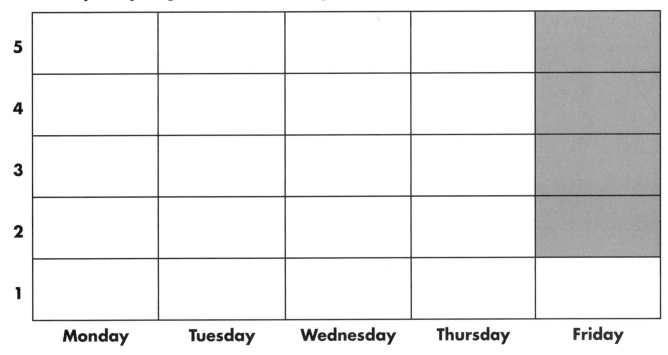

Daily Math Practice

Daily Progress Record 27

How many did you get correct each day? Color the squares.

	Monday	Tuesday	Wednesday	Thursday	Friday
5					
4					
3					
2					
1					

1. 140 – 40 = _____

2.   15
     + 45

3. Write the numbers in order.

290   300   280

_____ _____ _____

4. Make an **X** on the oval shape.

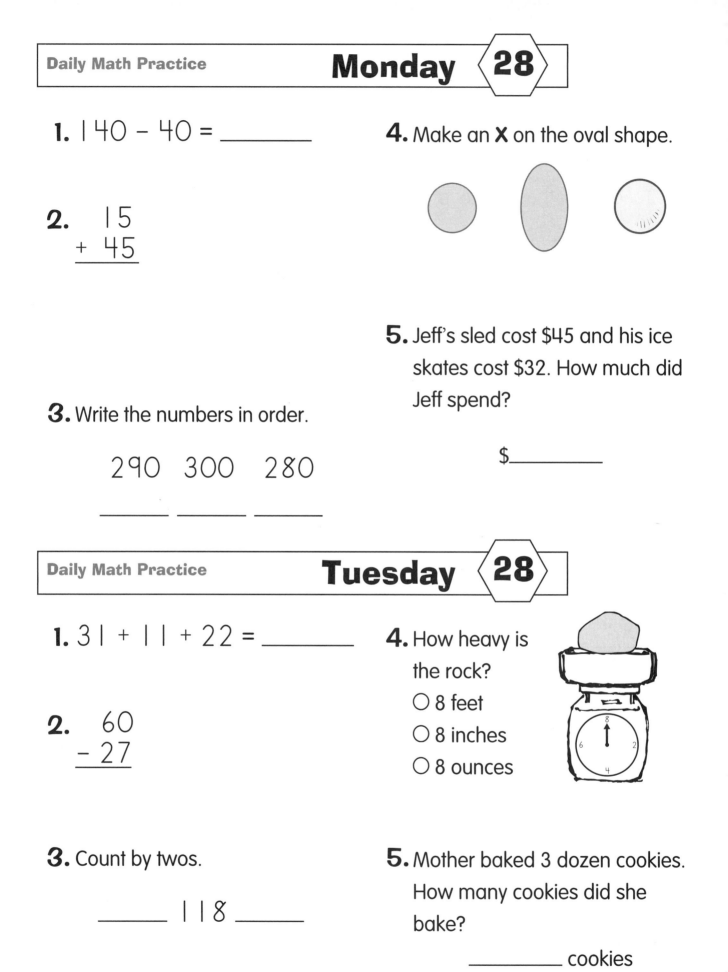

5. Jeff's sled cost $45 and his ice skates cost $32. How much did Jeff spend?

$_____

1. 31 + 11 + 22 = _____

2.   60
     – 27

3. Count by twos.

_____ 118 _____

4. How heavy is the rock?
○ 8 feet
○ 8 inches
○ 8 ounces

5. Mother baked 3 dozen cookies. How many cookies did she bake?

_____ cookies

1. $16 - 3 - 5 =$ _____

4. $24 + \boxed{} = 48$

2. $\begin{array}{r} 64 \\ + 9 \\ \hline \end{array}$

5. Dennis bought a bag of jelly beans. There were 23 green, 41 red, and 15 black jelly beans. How many jelly beans were in the bag?

_____ jelly beans

3. What is the perimeter?

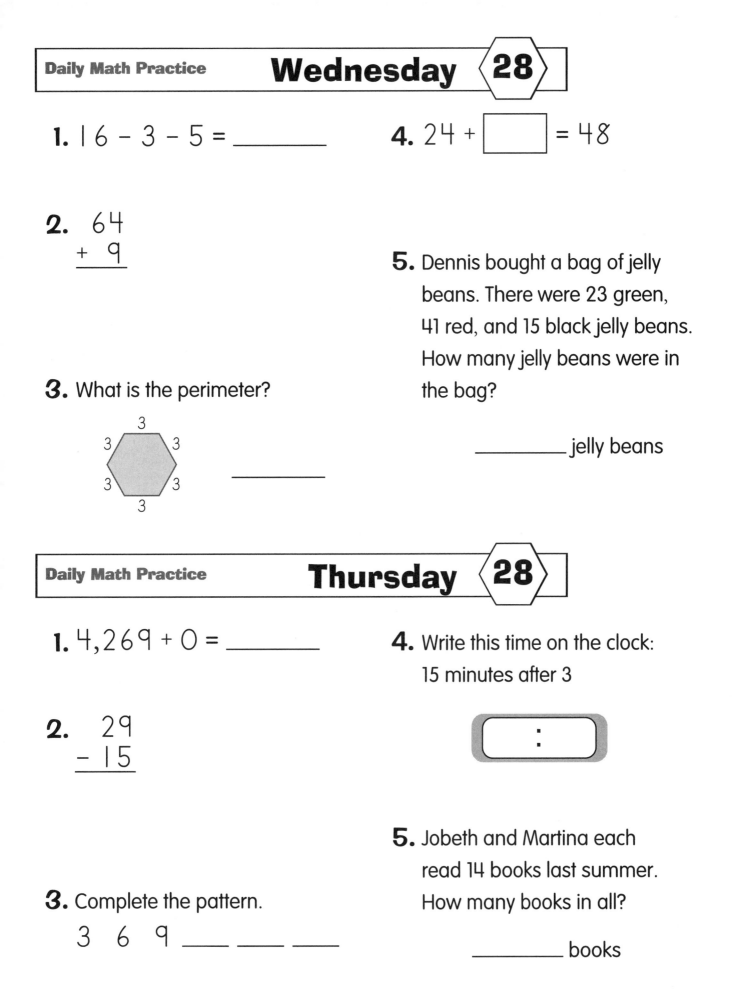

_____

1. $4,269 + 0 =$ _____

4. Write this time on the clock:
15 minutes after 3

[:]

2. $\begin{array}{r} 29 \\ - 15 \\ \hline \end{array}$

5. Jobeth and Martina each read 14 books last summer. How many books in all?

_____ books

3. Complete the pattern.

3   6   9   ___   ___   ___

Friday  28

Read the graph. Then answer the questions.

1. How many children wore shoes with:

Velcro® _____ buckles _____ shoelaces _____

2. What kind of shoe did most children wear?

    _____

3. What kind of shoe did the fewest children wear?

    _____

4. How many children are shown on the graph?

    _____

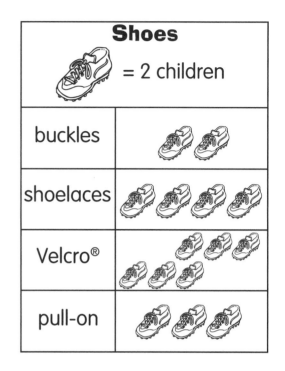

Shoes	= 2 children
buckles	
shoelaces	
Velcro®	
pull-on	

Daily Math Practice

Daily Progress Record ⟨28⟩

How many did you get correct each day? Color the squares.

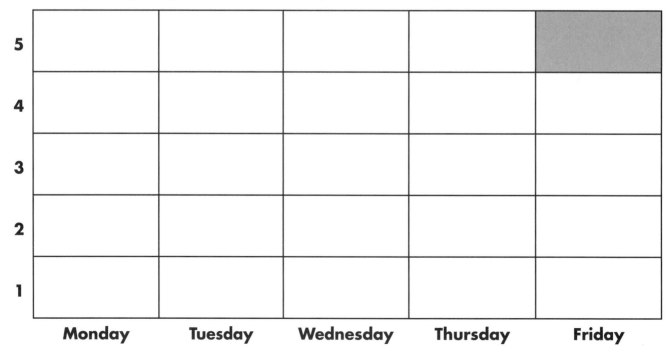

	Monday	Tuesday	Wednesday	Thursday	Friday
5					
4					
3					
2					
1					

1. 16 – 4 – 5 = _____

2. 37
     + 43

3. Mark the second letter.

R   B   X   J   Z   W

4. 182 =

____ hundred ____ tens

____ ones

5. For art class there are 12 each of blue, yellow, green, and red pencils. How many pencils are there in all?

_____ pencils

1. 4 + 4 + 4 + 4 = _____

2. 542
     – 542

3. Count by tens.

100 _____   160 _____
130 _____

4. Fill in the correct symbol.

< = >

pound ◯ ounce

5. There were 49 geese swimming in the pond, and then 23 flew away. How many were left?

_____ geese

1. $65 + 12 =$ _____

4. $6 + 4 = 5 +$ ☐

2. $\begin{array}{r} 42 \\ -\ 36 \\ \hline \end{array}$

5. Naomi wants an ice-cream cone with two scoops of ice cream. A scoop of ice cream is 30¢ and a cone is 25¢. How much will it cost?

_____ ¢

3. Color $\frac{1}{2}$.

☐ ☐ ☐ ☐ ☐
☐ ☐ ☐ ☐ ☐

---

1. $99 - 28 =$ _____

4. $15 -$ ☐ $= 9$

2. $\begin{array}{r} 223 \\ 104 \\ +\ 561 \\ \hline \end{array}$

5. What is half of 20? _____

Tell how you got that answer.

_____

_____

_____

3.  $=$ _____ ¢

How many feet do these goats have? Use the goat picture to help you.

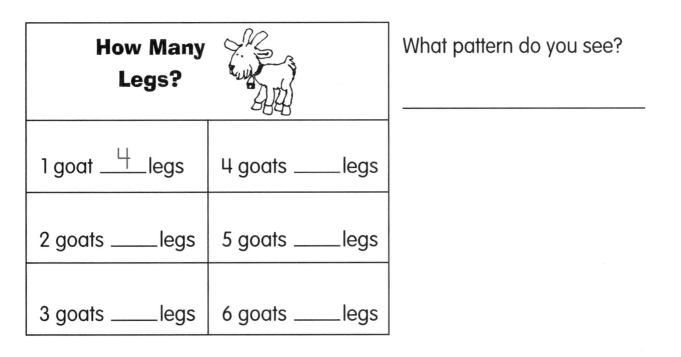

How Many Legs?	
1 goat __4__ legs	4 goats _____ legs
2 goats _____ legs	5 goats _____ legs
3 goats _____ legs	6 goats _____ legs

What pattern do you see?

_____

Daily Math Practice

Daily Progress Record ⟨29⟩

How many did you get correct each day? Color the squares.

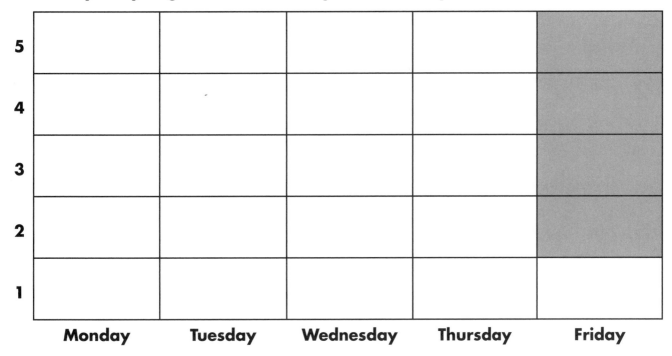

	Monday	Tuesday	Wednesday	Thursday	Friday
5					
4					
3					
2					
1					

1. 16 + 15 = _____

2. 175
    − 41

3. Write the numbers in order.

52 100 11 93 87

___ ___ ___ ___ ___

4. 5 is even.

        yes   no

5. Sheree found 46 shells and James found 25 shells. How many shells did they find?

_____ shells

1. 17 − 12 = _____

2. 63
    + 28

3. If half an hour is 30 minutes, how long is an hour?

_____ minutes

4. 9 + 6 = 6 + ☐

5. The Blue Jays had 68 points. The Red Birds had 26 points. Which team won the game?

_____

By how many points did they win?

_____ points

1. 32 − 19 = _____

2. 14
   + 9
   ‾‾‾‾

3. Mark the numbers that tell about money.

2¢ $5   5:00   10 cents   12 cm

4. 50 − 25 = 25, so

☐ + 25 = 50

5. A farmer has 4 pigs. Each pig has 6 piglets. How many piglets are there in all?

_____ piglets

---

1. 15 + 21 = _____

2. 32
   − 7
   ‾‾‾‾

3. Count by 5s.

20 ____   35 ____

50 ____   85 ____

4. Complete the pattern.

18 16 14 ___ ___

5. The movie started at 2:00. It lasted for 2 and a half hours. At what time did the movie end?

_____ : ____

Make the tally marks to show how many of each kind of flower.

Now color one space on the graph for each flower.

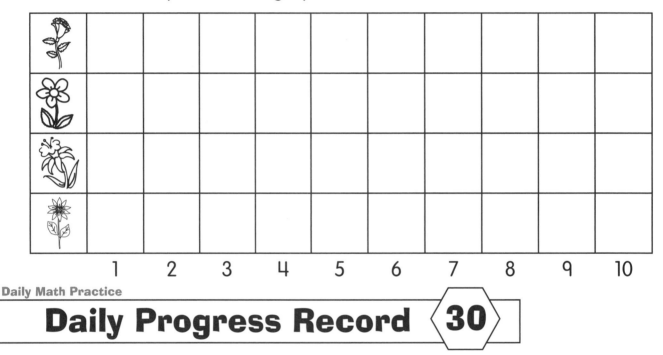

Daily Math Practice

Daily Progress Record   30

How many did you get correct each day? Color the squares.

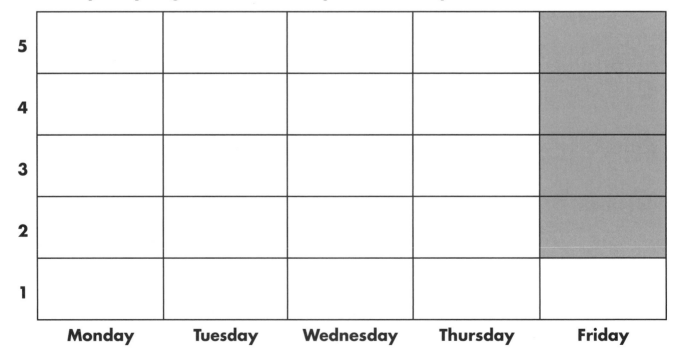

Monday  31

1. $18 - 5 =$ _____

2. $\begin{array}{r} 35 \\ + 41 \\ \hline \end{array}$

3. Name the shape.

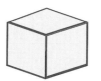

_____

4. Complete the pattern.

1 3 5 7 ___ ___ ___

5. Grandma bought a turkey. It cost $24. She gave the clerk $30. How much change did she get back?

$_____

Tuesday 31

1. $100 + 100 =$ _____

2. $\begin{array}{r} 60 \\ - 25 \\ \hline \end{array}$

3. Write the numbers in order.

58 52 50 54 56

___ ___ ___ ___ ___

4.   = $_____.

5. A fisherman caught 28 fish. He sold 18 fish and gave away 5 fish. How many did he have left?

_____ fish

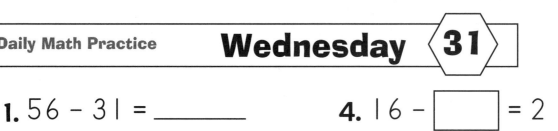

1. 56 − 31 = _____

4. 16 − [ ] = 2

2. 22
   34
  + 13
  _____

3. Draw a line of symmetry.

5. Angela earns $2 every week. She has saved her money for 8 weeks to buy a soccer ball. How much money does she have?

 $ _____

1. 13 + 48 = _____

4. 4 [ ] 3 = 12

2. 50
  − 43
  _____

3. Color $\frac{2}{4}$.

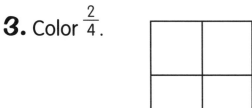

5. Matt baked 20 cupcakes. He and his friends ate half of the cupcakes. How many are left?

 _____ cupcakes

Circle the two sets of shapes that can be used to make a hexagon.

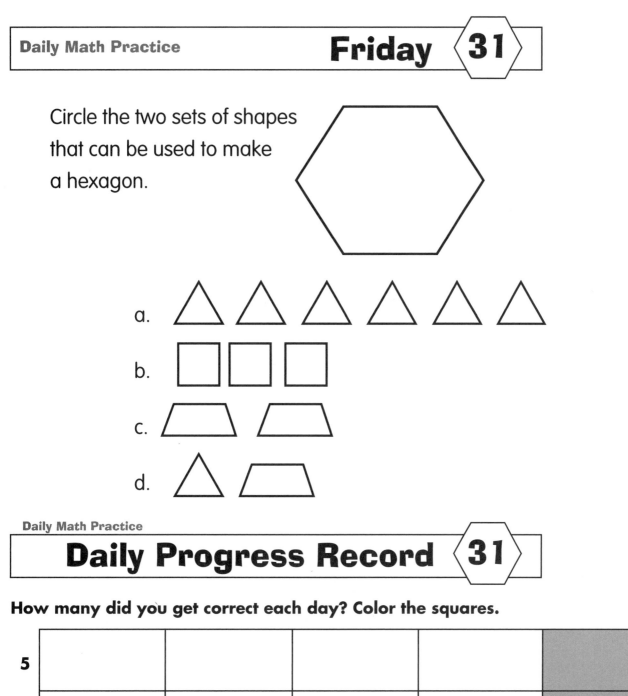

a.

b.

c.

d.

Daily Math Practice

Daily Progress Record 31

How many did you get correct each day? Color the squares.

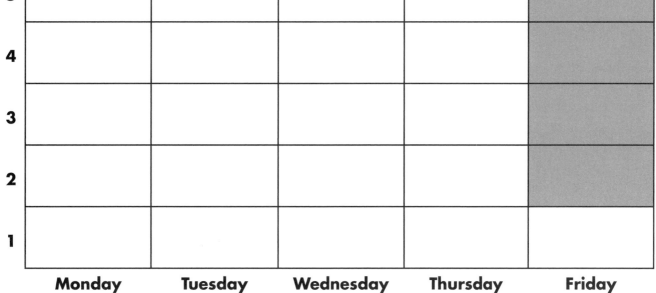

	Monday	Tuesday	Wednesday	Thursday	Friday
5					
4					
3					
2					
1					

1. $2 \times 2 =$ _____

2. $\begin{array}{r} 25 \\ -18 \\ \hline \end{array}$

3. What comes next?

489 _____   730 _____

554 _____

4. Write the number word for 13.

_____

5. Last year Christopher weighed 48 pounds. This year he weighs 60 pounds. How much weight has he gained?

_____ pounds

1. $16 + 18 =$ _____

2. $\begin{array}{r} 94 \\ -27 \\ \hline \end{array}$

3. What time is it?

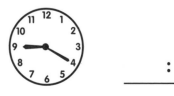

_____

4. $15 + 15 = 30$, so

$\boxed{} - 15 = 15$

5. Gina's father picked 12 oranges. He gave the same number of oranges to his four children. How many oranges did each one get?

_____ oranges

   EMC 751 • © Evan-Moor Corp.

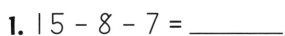

1. $15 - 8 - 7 =$ _____

2. $\begin{array}{r} 23 \\ + 21 \\ \hline \end{array}$

3. Fill in the correct symbol.

< = >

$100¢ \bigcirc \$1$

4. Circle the number that is the most likely to be picked without looking.

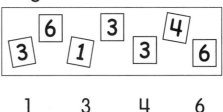

1   3   4   6

5. A quart of milk is equal to 4 cups. Mother used 3 quarts to make ice cream for the picnic. How many cups of milk did she use?

_____ cups

1. $4 \times 2 =$ _____

2. $\begin{array}{r} 61 \\ - 34 \\ \hline \end{array}$

3. Complete the pattern.

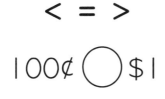 15 12 9 ___ ___

4. This is a sphere.

   yes   no

5. Jose opened his piggy bank. He found 2 quarters, 3 dimes, and 17 pennies. How much money did he have?

_____ ¢

Divide the cookies into 3 equal groups.

_____ in each group

How many did you get correct each day? Color the squares.

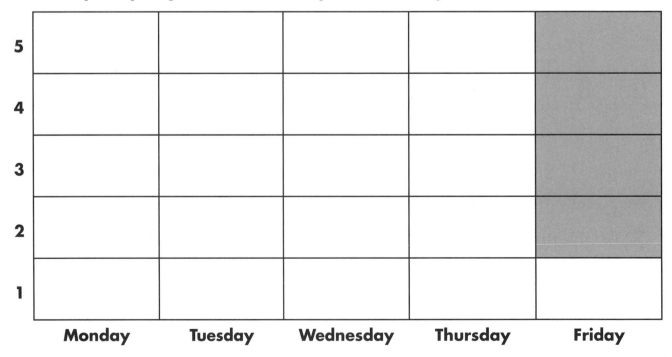

	Monday	Tuesday	Wednesday	Thursday	Friday
5					
4					
3					
2					
1					

1. 46 − 32 = _____

2. 810
      + 76

3. Show how 4 kids can share.

4. Write the numbers in order.

442 408 473 459

_____ _____ _____ _____

5. The bakery sold 31 pies on Sunday, 22 pies on Monday, and 16 pies on Tuesday. How many pies were sold in three days?

_____ pies

---

1. 5 × 2 = _____

2. 95
      − 38

3. Circle the names for 8.

4 + 4   16 − 8

12 − 5   4 × 2

4. Show 15 minutes after 5 on the clock.

5. If there are 8 legs on one spider, how many legs are on 5 spiders?

_____ legs

Wednesday ⟨**33**⟩

1. 76 – 30 = _____

4. Mark the ninth dot.

●●●●●●●●● ●

2.   53
      + 37
      ____

3. Which shape does NOT belong?

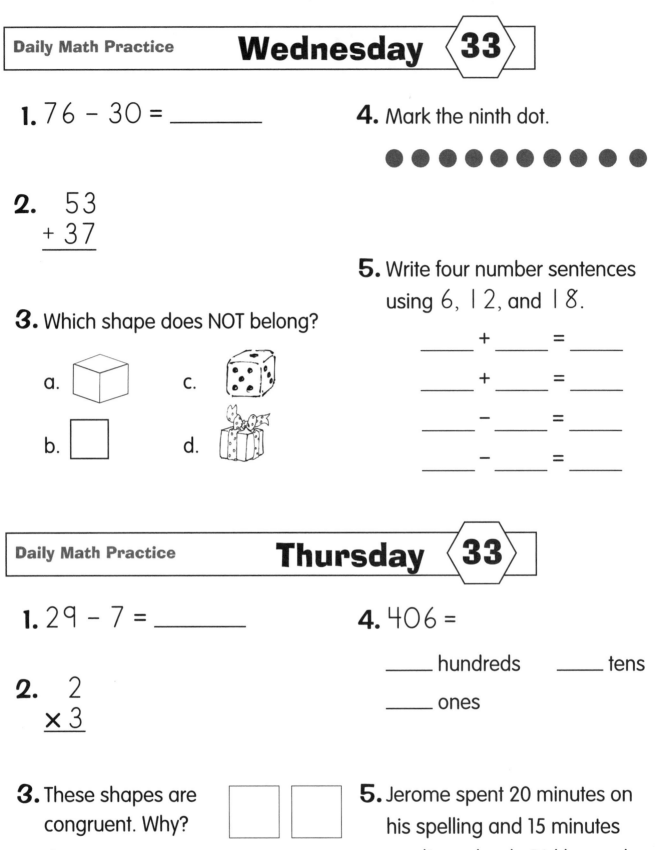

a.

c.

b.

d.

5. Write four number sentences using 6, 12, and 18.

_____ + _____ = _____

_____ + _____ = _____

_____ – _____ = _____

_____ – _____ = _____

Thursday ⟨**33**⟩

1. 29 – 7 = _____

2.   2
       × 3
      ____

4. 406 =

_____ hundreds   _____ tens

_____ ones

3. These shapes are congruent. Why?

○ same size, different shape

○ same size, same shape

○ different size, same shape

○ different size, different shape

5. Jerome spent 20 minutes on his spelling and 15 minutes reading a book. Did he work longer than a half hour?

yes   no

How much does your name cost?

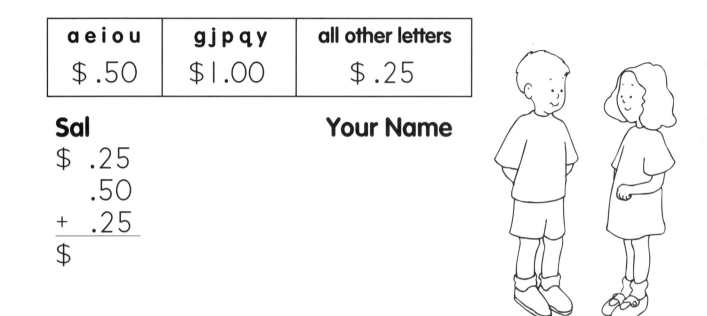

a e i o u	g j p q y	all other letters
$ .50	$1.00	$ .25

Sal

$ .25
   .50
+ .25
_____
$

Your Name

Daily Math Practice

Daily Progress Record ⟨33⟩

How many did you get correct each day? Color the squares.

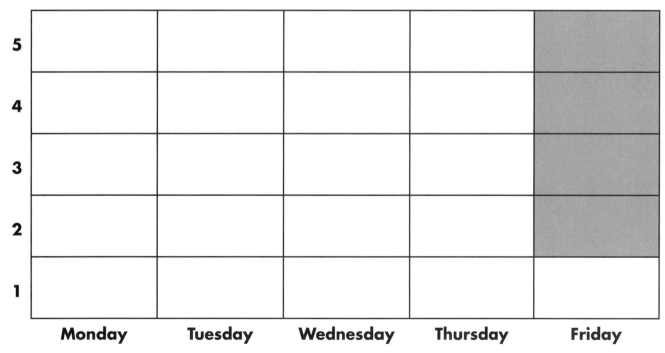

	Monday	Tuesday	Wednesday	Thursday	Friday
5					
4					
3					
2					
1					

Monday 34

1. $3 \times 3 =$ _____

2. $\begin{array}{r} 20 \\ + 70 \\ \hline \end{array}$

3. Write the numbers in order.

90 85 75 95 80

_____ _____ _____ _____ _____

4. Fill in the correct symbol.

$<\ =\ >$

fifteen $\bigcirc$ two + four

5. There are 23 grasshoppers, 106 ladybugs, and 210 ants in the backyard. How many insects are there?

_____ insects

Tuesday 34

1. $31 + 18 =$ _____

2. $\begin{array}{r} 62 \\ - 19 \\ \hline \end{array}$

3. Draw a shape with 5 sides and 5 corners.

4. $4 \times \square = 12$

5. Write a word problem for $16 - 14$.

_____

_____

_____

1. $5 \times 5 =$ _____

4. $15 + 24 = 24 +$ ⬚

2. $\begin{array}{r} 133 \\ + 126 \\ \hline \end{array}$

3. Fill in the correct symbol.

$$< \ = \ >$$

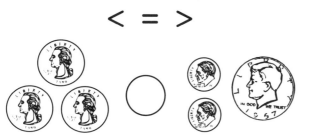

5. A group of 48 campers went on a hike. Soon 4 hikers got tired and stopped. Then 3 hikers got sick and stopped. How many campers made it to the end of the hike?

_____ campers

1. $66 - 32 =$ _____

4. $3 \times$ ⬚ $= 9$

2. $\begin{array}{r} 34 \\ + 49 \\ \hline \end{array}$

3. How long is the key?

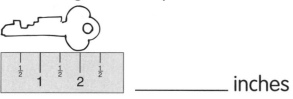

_____ inches

5. The party started at 3:00. It ended at 5:30 in the afternoon. How long did the party last?

_____ hours

How many coins do you need?

28¢	1			3
35¢				
49¢				

Daily Math Practice

Daily Progress Record 34

How many did you get correct each day? Color the squares.

	Monday	Tuesday	Wednesday	Thursday	Friday
5					
4					
3					
2					
1					

1. $2 \times 3 =$ _____

4. $25 \boxed{} 10 = 15$

2. $\begin{array}{r} 87 \\ + 13 \\ \hline \end{array}$

5. Today 253 students are eating a hot lunch and 106 brought lunch from home. How many students are eating lunch at school?

3. Divide the squares in half 4 different ways.

_____ students

---

1. $10 + 24 + 42 =$ _____

4. $13 + 12 = 25$, so

$$25 - \boxed{} = 12$$

2. $\begin{array}{r} 62 \\ - 27 \\ \hline \end{array}$

3. Count by tens.

140 _____ _____

_____ _____

5. It costs Sarah $10.77 a week to feed her pets. If she spends $6.52 on her dog, how much does she spend on her cat?

$_____

1. $2 \times 4 =$ _____

2. $\begin{array}{r} 473 \\ + 304 \\ \hline \end{array}$

3. Mark the clock that shows a quarter past 9.

4. Fill in the correct symbol.

$$< \quad = \quad >$$

$$0 \times 5 \bigcirc 9 \times 0$$

5. It is 469 miles to Uncle Ted's house. How far did Austin and Jordan travel today if they have 143 miles left to go?

_____ miles

1. $64 + 16 =$ _____

2. $\begin{array}{r} 629 \\ - 416 \\ \hline \end{array}$

3. $6 \div 2 =$ _____

4. Draw a shape with no corners.

5. Brian bought a pencil for 25¢. He paid for it with a half dollar. How much change did he get back?

a. 14¢   b. 50¢   c. 25¢

If I take one cookie without looking, what is the chance I'll get each of these cookies?

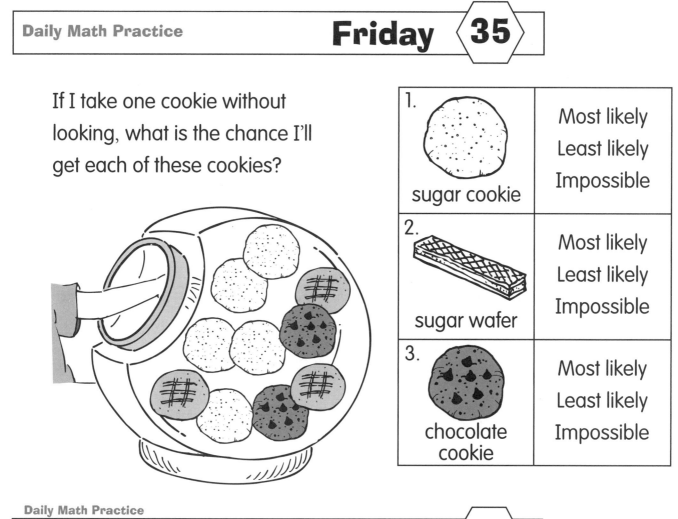

1. sugar cookie	Most likely Least likely Impossible
2. sugar wafer	Most likely Least likely Impossible
3. chocolate cookie	Most likely Least likely Impossible

Daily Math Practice

Daily Progress Record 〈35〉

How many did you get correct each day? Color the squares.

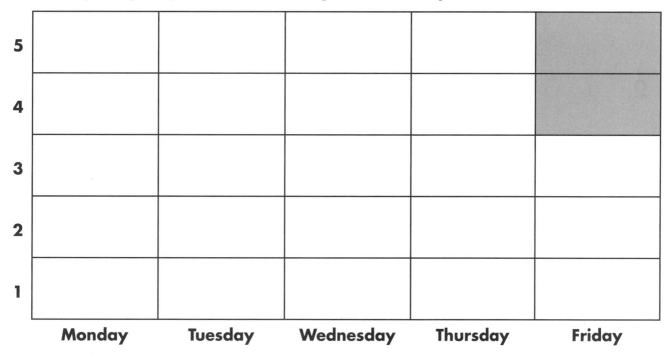

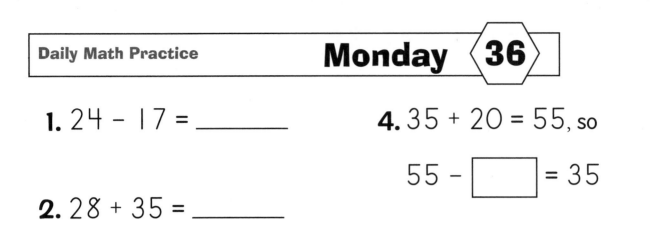

1. 24 − 17 = _____

2. 28 + 35 = _____

4. 35 + 20 = 55, so

55 − ☐ = 35

3. Write each number in the correct box.

1 9 2 8 3 4 10 5 7 6

Even	Odd

5. Tom is building a tepee. He bought 167 nails and used 94. How many nails were left?

_____ nails

1. 3 × 4 = _____

2.
```
  14
  64
+ 23
```

4. Fill in the correct symbol.

< = >

900 ◯ 899

3. How many sides does a cube have?

_____ sides

5. A new bike costs $137. Carolina has saved $84. How much more does she need?

$_____

1. 40 + 18 = _____

2. 50
       − 22
       ____

3. What time will it be in 30 minutes?

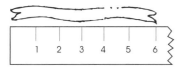

a. 4:00 c. 4:15
b. 4:30 d. 4:45

4. Estimate.

250 + 375 =
a. 600 b. 125 c. 5,000

5. After the soccer game, the team went to Kelly's house. They ate 27 cookies and 16 brownies. How many snacks did the team eat?

_____ snacks

---

1. 3 × 5 = _____

2.   123
       + 635
       ____

3. How long is the ribbon?

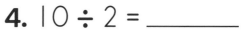

_____ cm

4. 10 ÷ 2 = _____

5. Last Saturday, 128 adults and 164 children went to the ball game. How many people were at the game?

_____ people

Friday ⬡36⬡

Tomas ate $\frac{1}{2}$ of the jelly beans. Lisa ate $\frac{1}{4}$ of the jelly beans. If there were 20 jelly beans, how many did they eat?

Tomas _____   Lisa _____

How many jelly beans were left?

_____ jelly beans

Daily Progress Record ⬡36⬡

How many did you get correct each day? Color the squares.

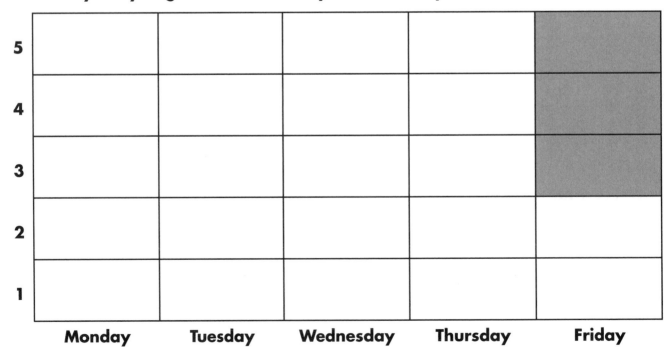

	Monday	Tuesday	Wednesday	Thursday	Friday
5					
4					
3					
2					
1					

How to Solve
Word Problems

✓ Read the problem carefully. Think about what it says.

✓ Look for clue words. The clue words will tell you if you should add or subtract.

✓ Solve the problem.

✓ Check your work. Make sure your answer makes sense.

Clue Words

Add	Subtract
in all	more than
altogether	less than
total	are left
sum	take away
both	difference
plus	fewer

Monday
1. 2
2. 9
3. The second ball should be marked.
4. 8, 4, 2
5. 10 fish

Tuesday
1. 6
2. 10
3. 20¢
4. 7
5. 3 more ate cake

Wednesday
1. 0
2. 8
3. a, b, d
4. 6:30 OR half past 6
5. 4¢

Thursday
1. 6
2. 9
3. The ball and sphere should be marked.
4. 10, 20, 30, 40, 50
5. 6 toy animals

Friday
1. 7:00–1   5:30–3   6:00–7
2. 6
3. Answers will vary.

Week **2**

Monday
1. 7
2. 10
3. 50¢
4. 28, 29, 30, 31, 32
5. 3 + 2 = 5 or 2 + 3 = 5
   5 – 3 = 2 or 5 – 2 = 3

Tuesday
1. 9
2. 10
3. 30 fingers
4. 7
5. 9 blocks

Wednesday
1. 9
2. 5
3. 20
4. rectangle
5. 4 apples

Thursday
1. 1
2. 10
3. 4:30
4. X O
5. 4 horses

Friday
$7, $3

Week **3**

Monday
1. 9
2. 4
3. The fifth flower should be marked.
4. 4 + 6 = 10
5. 40 cents

Tuesday
1. 10
2. 4
3. 33, 58, 100
4. The half apple should be marked.
5. 5 fireflies

Wednesday
1. 9
2. 1
3. 12
4. A
5. 3 jelly beans

Thursday
1. 0
2. 9
3. 13 marbles
4. 70, 80, 90, 100
5. 2 cookies

Friday
3 + 4 = 7, 4 + 3 = 7, 7 – 4 = 3,
7 – 3 = 4

Monday
1. 11
2. 6
3. One section should be colored.
4. 28, 29, 30, 31, 32
5. 6 bananas were left

Tuesday
1. 1
2. 11
3. 30, 70, 100
4. 12 − 8 = 4
5. 6 things

Wednesday
1. 10
2. 3
3. 27 < 41
4. 18¢
5. 7 horses

Thursday
1. 2
2. 12
3. circle
4. 5 should be circled.
5. 17 points

Friday
12, yes

Monday
1. 3
2. 12
3. 64 > 48
4. 6 should be circled.
5. Answers will vary.

Tuesday
1. 6
2. 12
3. 20, 22, 24, 26, 28, 30
4. The two squares should be marked.
5. 13 balloons

Wednesday
1. 11
2. 5
3. yes
4. 99, 100, 101, 102, 103
5. 2

Thursday
1. 11
2. 4
3. 23
4. 3 inches
5. 5 apples

Friday

Monday
1. 11
2. 8
3. A, D, and E should be marked.
4. 120, 130
5. 11 vegetables

Tuesday
1. 10
2. 11
3. Two buttons should be colored.
4. 6
5. Answers will vary.

Wednesday
1. 9
2. 12
3. ten, sixteen
4. 6 o'clock
5. 4 yellow apples

Thursday
1. 9
2. 12
3. 5 + 5, 3 + 7, 6 + 4, 8 + 2
4. The lion should be marked.
5. 5 baskets

Friday
3 more loaves

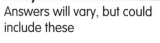

Monday
1. 15
2. 8
3. The sixth ant should be marked.
4. no
5. 2 hours

Tuesday
1. 15
2. 6
3. 33, 58, 80
4. 20, 18, 16, 14, 12, 10
5. 3 kittens

Wednesday
1. 6
2. 13
3. 34
4. A possible pattern:

5. 14 ribbons

Thursday
1. 9
2. 15
3. gallon
4. 7 + 5 = 12
5. 8 steps

Friday
Answers will vary, but could include these

Monday
1. 9
2. 12
3. 57¢
4. 6 + 6 = 12
5. Answers will vary.

Tuesday
1. 0
2. 14
3. All but the button should be marked.
4. 11, 12, 20
5. 14 chickens

Wednesday
1. 15
2. 9
3. 6 cm
4. 12
5. 8 + 5

Thursday
1. 10
2. 4
3. no
4. yes
5. $1

Friday
Answers will vary.

Monday
1. 15
2. 9
3. 25¢
4. 97, 96, 95, 94, 93, 92, 91
5. 14 mittens

Tuesday
1. 4
2. 13
3. 20
4. 12 + 4 = 4 + 12
5. 8 + 7 = 15, 7 + 8 = 15, 15 − 8 = 7, 15 − 7 = 8

Wednesday
1. 9
2. 20
3. ABBABBABB
4. 2, 4, 6
5. none is left OR 0 is left

Thursday
1. 15
2. 7
3. 14
4. 8, 80
5. yes

Friday
Possible combinations:
red, blue   red, yellow
blue, yellow

blue, red   yellow, blue
yellow, red

red, red   blue, blue
yellow, yellow

Monday
1. 9
2. 15
3. 6 + 6, 3 + 9, 5 + 7
4. no
5. 8

Tuesday
1. 9
2. 12
3. half past 8
4. yes
5. 8 more elephants

Wednesday
1. 100
2. 14
3. over __3__ up __2__
4. The circle with one section shaded should be marked.
5. 15 books

Thursday
1. twelve
2. 9
3. 12 pounds
4. 47
5. 5 – 3 = 2

Friday
twelve
Individual problems will vary.

Monday
1. seven
2. 9
3. 55¢
4. 6 + 7 = 7 + 6
5. 2 boxes of cookies

Tuesday
1. 7 + 7 = 14
2. 17
3. 40, 50, 60, 70, 80
4. 13
5. 11 cans

Wednesday
1. 17
2. 9
3. 6, 12
   20, 18
4. 15 – 8 = 7
5. square

Thursday
1. 4
2. Answers will vary, but must equal 14.
3. A triangle should be drawn.
4. 9
5. 10

Friday
10 blocks in one day, 50 blocks in five days

Monday
1. ten
2. 14
3. Any four combinations that equal 14.
4. $\frac{2}{4}$
5. 13 people

Tuesday
1. 11
2. 5
3. The clock face should show 2:00.
4. 98, 99, 100, 101, 102, 103
5. 7 minutes

Wednesday
1. 5
2. 16
3. The two clocks should be marked.
4. 46 < 48
5. 7 fish

Thursday
1. 12
2. 10
3. The second shape should be marked.
4. 40, 45, 50
5. 8 more eggs

Friday
13, Oscar

Monday
1. sixteen
2. 9
3. 73¢
4. 9 + 7 = 7 + 9
5. 15 sea lions

Tuesday
1. 0
2. 6
3. The cone should be marked.
4. 1, 3, 5, 7, and 9 should be marked.
5. 7 pigeons

Wednesday
1. 17
2. 26
3. The two sides should be symmetrical.
4. 108, 109, 110, 111, 112
5. 15 miles

Thursday
1. 15
2. 17
3. c
4. The third object should be circled.
5. 15 trees

Friday

trunk	1	2	5
ears	2	4	10
feet	4	8	20
tail	1	2	5

Week 14

Monday
1. 7
2. 10
3. 18 feet
4. 11 + 2 = 13
5. 7 minutes

Tuesday
1. 9
2. 37
3. The fourth slipper should be marked.
4. 12
5. 13 rows

Wednesday
1. 17
2. 4
3. 50
4. ABCABC
5. 10 animals

Thursday
1. 0
2. 12
3. half past 11
4. 4 + 5 > 6 − 2
5. 2 flowers

Friday
12 shoes

Week 15

Monday
1. 16
2. 12
3. 19 should be marked.
4. 15 minutes
5. 15 eggs

Tuesday
1. 14
2. 15
3. 11
4. no
5. Answers will vary.

Wednesday
1. 7
2. 49
3. 110, 111, 112, 113
4. 卌 卌 卌 卌 卌 ////
5. 11 friends

Thursday
1. 10
2. 10
3. 20, 50, 90
4. six
5. 11 + 6 = 17

Friday

1	2	3
4	2	0
1	2	3

Monday
1. 14
2. 9
3.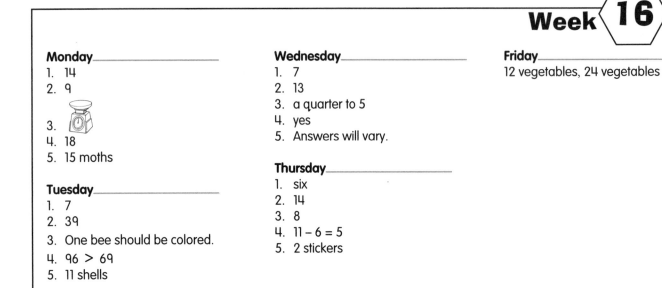
4. 18
5. 15 moths

Tuesday
1. 7
2. 39
3. One bee should be colored.
4. 96 > 69
5. 11 shells

Wednesday
1. 7
2. 13
3. a quarter to 5
4. yes
5. Answers will vary.

Thursday
1. six
2. 14
3. 8
4. 11 – 6 = 5
5. 2 stickers

Friday
12 vegetables, 24 vegetables

Monday
1. 15
2. 7
3. The seventh balloon should be marked.
4. 16
5. 7 children

Tuesday
1. 39
2. 9
3. $\frac{1}{3}$
4. c
5. no

Wednesday
1. 17
2. 22
3. 96, 99
   130, 159
4. six
5. 15 + 4 =

Thursday
1. 26
2. 5
3. The cube should be marked.
4. 5, 10, 15, 20, 25, 30
5. less than $1

Friday
Answers will vary, but must be true statements about the graph.

Monday
1. 16
2. 62
3. 12 o'clock
4. 12
5. 18

Tuesday
1. 4
2. 27
3. 62, 64, 66, 68, 70
4. Objects will vary, but must be in an AABBAABB pattern.
5. 6 cupcakes

Wednesday
1. 17
2. 8
3. c
4. 8 + 7 > 12 – 3
5. b

Thursday
1. 19
2. 9
3. yes
4. 11 + 6 = 17
5. c

Friday
Pictures will vary, but must follow the pattern.

Monday
1. 16
2. 7
3. 90, 76
   130, 112
4. 130, 160, 200
5. 6¢

Tuesday
1. 9
2. 14
3. The bread slice should be divided in half.
4. six
5. 9 years

Wednesday
1. 13
2. 9
3. 2, 3, 1 OR truck, car, bike
4. 24
5. 65¢

Thursday
1. 5
2. 69
3. ABBCABBC
4. no
5. 9 stamps

Friday

| | over | 4 | | over | 2 |
| | up | 3 | | up | 2 |

Monday
1. 8
2. 89
3. 90, 68, 46
4. 305 > 159
5. 8 students

Tuesday
1. 28
2. three
3. $2\frac{1}{2}$ inches
4. 12 + 12 = 24
5. 8 + 9 = 17, 9 + 8 = 17, 17 − 9 = 8, 17 − 8 = 9

Wednesday
1. 4
2. 19
3. 17
4. 9, 3
5. 8 toy cars

Thursday
1. 18
2. 2
3. The clock should show 3:30.
4. One section should be colored.
5. 9 saddles

Friday
5 hammers, 50 nails, 20 pieces of lumber

Monday
1. 5
2. 24
3. The fourth candy cane should be marked.
4. eight = six + two
5. $3

Tuesday
1. 7
2. 38
3. 20, 25, 30, 35, 40
4. quarter past 7
5. 5 friends

Wednesday
1. 12
2. 100
3. ABCCABCC
4. 10 + 8 < 9 + 10
5. Any four combinations that equal 13.

Thursday
1. 23
2. 24
3. 4 tens and 2 ones = 42
4. 8 dimes
5. more than 10

Friday

1 kid	10	6 kids	60
2 kids	20	7 kids	70
3 kids	30	8 kids	80
4 kids	40	9 kids	90
5 kids	50	10 kids	100

counting by 10 OR adding 10 each time

Monday
1. 17
2. 113
3. 3, 6, 9, 11, 20
4. 12
5.

1 hour ago	now	1 hour later
2:15	3:15	4:15
6:45	7:45	8:45
10:30	11:30	12:30

Tuesday
1. 10
2. 70¢
3. The sphere should be marked.
4. The student should draw any quadrilateral.
5. a

Wednesday
1. 9
2. 394
3. 4:45
4. 0
5. 77¢

Thursday
1. 18
2. 44
3. 15
4. $12 - 3 = 9$
5. 17 books

Friday
14 squares

Monday
1. 11
2. 28
3. 4, 10
4. 10
5. 40¢

Tuesday
1. 18
2. 78
3. 100, 102, 104, 106, 108, 110
4. 100
5. 4 pairs of shoes

Wednesday
1. 96
2. 11
3. $\frac{3}{4}$
4. 50¢
5. 18 insects

Thursday
1. 40
2. 37
3. liter bottle < gallon carton
4. 87
5. 16 animals

Friday
Answers will vary.

9¢		1	4
11¢	1		1
16¢	1	1	1
24¢	2		4

Monday
1. 21
2. 48
3. 130, 100
   190, 170
4. 9
5. 18

Tuesday
1. 41¢
2. 12
3. fifteen
4. 19
5. The clock face should show 2:30.

Wednesday
1. 10
2. 546
3. 5, 5
4. twelve > two
5. 22 hippos

Thursday
1. 9
2. 66
3. Pictures will vary.
4. $1.00
5. 13 monkeys

Friday
60 marbles, 20 marbles

Week 25

Monday
1. 47
2. 212
3. 166, 167, 168, 169, 170
4. 10 + 6 = 16
5. 44 years

Tuesday
1. 80
2. 31
3. Gallon, liter, and quart should be marked.
4. 60 minutes
5. 24¢

Wednesday
1. 6
2. 31
3. different size
4. 0
5. The clock should show 6:15.

Thursday
1. 5
2. 653
3. first–A OR circle, last–C OR triangle
4.
5. 14 eggs

Friday
Sphere: A, C, E; Circle: B, D, F
Individual drawings will vary.

Week 26

Monday
1. 10
2. 28
3. Answers will vary, but must be an odd number.
4. sixteen < nineteen
5. 12 chickens

Tuesday
1. 67
2. 17
3. 6:30
4. 6 tens and 4 ones
5. 13 more boys

Wednesday
1. 24
2. 35
3. 75, 80, 85, 90, 95
4. 30 – 10 = 20
5. Answers will vary.

Thursday
1. 39
2. 40
3. 14, 17
4. 16
5. 21 candles

Friday
Pictures will vary.

Week 27

Monday
1. 90
2. 423
3. 216 < 261
4. eighteen — 20
   thirteen — 18
   twenty — 12
   twelve — 13
5. 34 cards

Tuesday
1. 5,893
2. 657
3. cone

4. Answers will vary, but must be an even number.
5. 85¢

Wednesday
1. 28
2. 12
3. $\frac{1}{4}$
4. 120
5. 40¢

Thursday
1. 0
2. 81
3. 8 cm
4. 2 quarters
5. 16 wheels

Friday
9

Monday
1. 100
2. 60
3. 280, 290, 300
4. The oval should be marked.
5. $77

Tuesday
1. 64
2. 33
3. 116, 118, 120
4. 8 ounces
5. 36 cookies

Wednesday
1. 8
2. 73
3. 18
4. 24 + 24 = 48
5. 79 jelly beans

Thursday
1. 4,269
2. 14
3. 12, 15, 18
4. The clock should show 3:15.
5. 28 books

Friday
1. Velcro®–12, buckles–4, shoelaces–8
2. Velcro®
3. buckles
4. 30

Monday
1. 7
2. 80
3. B should be marked.
4. 1 hundred, 8 tens, 2 ones
5. 48 pencils

Tuesday
1. 16
2. 0
3. 110, 170, 140
4. pound > ounce
5. 26 geese

Wednesday
1. 77
2. 6
3. Five boxes should be colored.
4. 6 + 4 = 5 + 5
5. 85¢

Thursday
1. 71
2. 888
3. 50¢
4. 15 – 6 = 9
5. 10
Answers will vary, but could include:
"I drew 20 sticks and marked half of them. Then I counted what I marked."
"I know that 20 is 10 + 10, so half is 10."

Friday

4	16
8	20
12	24

counting by 4s OR adding 4 every time

Monday
1. 31
2. 134
3. 11, 52, 87, 93, 100
4. no
5. 71 shells

Tuesday
1. 5
2. 91
3. 60 minutes
4. 9 + 6 = 6 + 9
5. Blue Jays, 42 points

Wednesday
1. 13
2. 23
3. 2¢, $5, 10 cents
4. 25
5. 24 piglets

Thursday
1. 36
2. 25
3. 25, 40 55, 90
4. 12, 10
5. 4:30

Friday

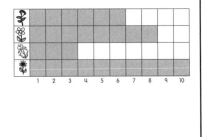

Monday
1. 13
2. 76
3. cube
4. 9, 11, 13
5. $6

Tuesday
1. 200
2. 35
3. 50, 52, 54, 56, 58
4. $1.30
5. 5 fish

Wednesday
1. 25
2. 69
3. A correct line of symmetry should be drawn.
4. 16 – 14 = 2
5. $16

Thursday
1. 61
2. 7
3. Two sections should be colored.
4. 4 x 3 = 12
5. 10 cupcakes

Friday
a. △ △ △ △ △
c. ▱ ▱

Monday
1. 4
2. 7
3. 490, 731, 555
4. thirteen
5. 12 pounds

Tuesday
1. 34
2. 67
3. 9:20
4. 30
5. 3 oranges

Wednesday
1. 0
2. 44
3. 100¢ = $1
4. 3
5. 12 cups

Thursday
1. 8
2. 27
3. 6, 3
4. yes
5. 97¢

Friday
4 in each group

Monday
1. 14
2. 886
3. The cookies should be divided into 4 sets of 2.
4. 408, 442, 459, 473
5. 69 pies

Tuesday
1. 10
2. 57
3. 4 + 4, 16 – 8, 4 x 2
4. The clock should show 5:15.
5. 40 legs

Wednesday
1. 46
2. 90
3. b
4. The ninth dot should be marked.
5. 6 + 12 = 18, 12 + 6 = 18, 18 – 6 = 12, 18 – 12 = 6

Thursday
1. 22
2. 6
3. same size, same shape
4. 4 hundreds, 0 tens, 6 ones
5. yes

Friday
$1.00
Individual answers will vary.

Monday
1. 9
2. 90
3. 75, 80, 85, 90, 95
4. fifteen > two + four
5. 339 insects

Tuesday
1. 49
2. 43
3. Students should draw any 5-sided polygon.
4. 4 x 3 = 12
5. Answers will vary.

Wednesday
1. 25
2. 259
3.  >
4. 15
5. 41 campers

Thursday
1. 34
2. 83
3. $2\frac{1}{2}$ inches
4. 3 x 3 = 9
5. $2\frac{1}{2}$ hours OR 2 hours and 30 minutes

Friday
Answers will vary.

	(img)	(img)	(img)	(img)
28¢	1			3
35¢	1	1		
49¢	1	1	2	4

Monday
1. 6
2. 100
3. The squares should be divided in half four different ways.
4. 25 – 10 = 15
5. 359 students

Tuesday
1. 76
2. 35
3. 140, 150, 160, 170, 180
4. 13
5. $4.25

Wednesday
1. 8
2. 777
3. The second clock should be marked.
4. 0 x 5 = 9 x 0
5. 326 miles

Thursday
1. 80
2. 213
3. 3
4. Answers will vary.
5. c

Friday
1. Most likely
2. Impossible
3. Least likely

Monday
1. 7
2. 63
3. Even: 2, 8, 4, 10, 6
   Odd: 1, 9, 3, 5, 7
4. 20
5. 73 nails

Tuesday
1. 12
2. 101
3. 6 sides
4. 900 > 899
5. $53

Wednesday
1. 58
2. 28
3. c
4. a
5. 43 snacks

Thursday
1. 15
2. 758
3. 6 cm
4. 5
5. 292 people

Friday
Tomas–10, Lisa–5
5 jelly beans